The Rapture
Fact or Fiction?

The Rapture
Fact or Fiction?

Dr. David R. Reagan

LAMB
& LION
MINISTRIES
McKinney, Texas

Dedicated to

Tim Moore

My friend, colleague and designated successor
who has a passion for the Lord's soon return.

First edition, 2019

Copyright © 2019 by Lamb & Lion Ministries

ISBN: 978-0-945593-31-7

Library of Congress Control Number: 2019900022

Lamb & Lion Ministries
P.O. Box 919
McKinney, Texas 75070
lamblion@lamblion.com
www.lamblion.com

Cover design by Trey Collich.

All scripture quotations, unless otherwise noted, are from the *New
American Standard Version*, © 1995 by the Lockman Foundation.

Printed in the United States of America.

Contents

Books by Dr. David R. Reagan

The Christ in Prophecy Study Guide (McKinney, TX: Lamb & Lion Ministries, 1987). Second edition in 2001; third edition in 2006.

Trusting God: Learning to Walk by Faith (Lafayette, LA: Huntington House, 1987). Second edition in 1994; third edition in 2015.

Jesus is Coming Again! (Eugene, OR: Harvest House, 1992).

The Master Plan: Making Sense of the Controversies Surrounding Bible Prophecy Today (Eugene, OR: Harvest House, 1993).

Living for Christ in the End Times (Green Forest, AR: New Leaf Press, 2000). Second edition in 2015.

Wrath and Glory: Unveiling the Majestic Book of Revelation (Green Forest, AR: New Leaf Press, 2001). Second edition in 2016.

America the Beautiful? The United States in Bible Prophecy (McKinney, TX: Lamb & Lion Ministries, 2003). Second edition in 2006; third edition in 2009.

God's Plan for the Ages: The Blueprint of Bible Prophecy (McKinney, TX: Lamb & Lion Ministries, 2005).

Eternity: Heaven or Hell? (McKinney, TX: Lamb & Lion Ministries, 2010).

Jesus: The Lamb and The Lion (McKinney, TX: Lamb & Lion Ministries, 2011).

The Man of Lawlessness: The Antichrist in the Tribulation (McKinney, TX: Lamb & Lion Ministries, 2012).

A Prophetic Manifesto (McKinney, TX: Lamb & Lion Ministries, 2012).

Living on Borrowed Time: The Imminent Return of Jesus (McKinney, TX: Lamb & Lion Ministries, 2013).

The Jewish People: Rejected or Beloved? (McKinney, TX: Lamb & Lion Ministries, 2014).

Israel in Bible Prophecy: Past, Present & Future (McKinney, TX: Lamb & Lion Ministries, 2017).

God's Prophetic Voices to America (McKinney, TX: Lamb & Lion Ministries, 2017).

The Basics of Bible Prophecy (McKinney, TX: Lamb & Lion Ministries, 2018). Written together with Darryl Nunnelley.

Preface

Why another book on the Rapture? After all, there are many excellent books on the topic.[1] But most are either theological in nature, or else they are so detailed that you can't see the forest for the trees.

The purpose of this book is to reach out to the general public — to those who know little or nothing about the Rapture. And, hopefully, it will also supply very usable material for Bible prophecy teachers who desire to teach the fundamentals about the Rapture to folks who know little about the subject.

The Rapture is one of the Lord's most precious promises to the Church. When the Apostle Paul described it in detail in 1 Thessalonians 4:13-18, he concluded his description by saying, "Therefore, comfort one another with these words" (1 Thessalonians 4:18).

Yet, the concept of the Rapture and its details are completely unknown to most professing Christians — both Catholic and Protestant. And that is a tragedy.

Hopefully, this book will be used by the Lord to open many eyes to the marvelous promise of the Rapture and the hope it provides.

Maranatha!

Dave Reagan

Allen, Texas
February 2019

Midnight Cry

A song by Chuck and Greg Day
© Bridge Building Music (BMI)

I hear the sound of a mighty rushing wind,
And it's closer now than it's ever been.
I can almost hear the trumpet
As Gabriel sounds the call.
At the midnight cry,
We'll be going home.

I look around me;
I see prophecies fulfilled.
The signs of the times,
They're appearing everywhere.
I can almost hear the Father
Tell the Son, "Go get my children."
At the midnight cry,
The Bride of Christ shall rise.

Chorus:
When Jesus steps out
On a cloud to call His children,
The dead in Christ shall rise
To meet Him in the air.
And then those that remain
Shall be quickly changed.
At the midnight cry,
Jesus comes again.

Part 1

The Concept

Iwas born in 1938 and grew up in the 1940s and 50s. I was blessed to be born into a devout Christian family, and I literally grew up in the Church. I was there every time the doors were open — Sunday mornings and evenings, Wednesday evenings, Gospel meetings and Vacation Bible School. Yet, despite all this exposure to biblical teaching, I was 30 years old before I heard about the Rapture — and it wasn't from my church.

This amazing biblical ignorance was due to the fact that I grew up during a time when a person could be religiously isolated. There was no such thing as Christian bookstores, and Christian radio programs were few and far between. We did not have access to television until 1955, the beginning of my senior year in high school.

To make matters worse, my family was a member of a Christian sect that believed it was the one and only true church, and we were constantly warned against reading any materials produced by "the denominations." Complicating matters further for me was the fact that my church was militantly Amillennial, so our preachers spiritualized all that the Bible had to say about the end times and the Second Coming.[2]

To say the least, it is a miracle of God that I ended up being a Bible prophecy teacher with a Premillennial viewpoint.

Discovering the Rapture

So, after attending church faithfully for 30 years, if you had asked me to define the Rapture, I would probably have responded by saying, "It's a sensation you feel when your girlfriend kisses you."

The first time I heard about the biblical concept of the Rapture was when a person handed me a rather crude brochure with a picture that depicted cars crashing into each other and planes flying into buildings. Jesus was portrayed in the sky with outstretched arms, and people were shown on earth emerging from graves in white robes.

I was completely perplexed by it all. I thought it had been produced by some cult. But then, when I looked at the end of the brochure, I saw the name of a local Baptist church.

That was over 50 years ago, and ignorance of the Rapture is still widespread within Christendom. Among the few non-Christians who are aware of what it is, there is mainly derision and mocking, such as was contained in the ridiculous horror-comedy movie, *Rapture-Palooza.*[3]

Christian Mockery

Tragically, a lot of the mockery today originates within the Church from people who believe the Rapture is an Alice-in-Wonderland product of the imaginations of Fundamentalist Christians who really know little or nothing about the Bible.

A British magazine, *Christian Today*, recently printed an article titled, "Why A Zombie Invasion Is More Likely Than A Religious Apocalypse."[4] Each year when prophecy teacher Jan Markell of Olive Tree Ministries in Minnesota holds the largest Bible prophecy conference in the nation, critics within Christianity give it derisive names like, "Jan Markell's End Time Hysteria Conference."[5]

Much of this mockery is motivated by the fact that there

have been so many irresponsible Bible prophecy teachers over the years who have set dates for the Rapture. You might remember, for example, Edgar Whisenant who published a pamphlet back in the 1980s that was titled, "88 Reasons Why the Rapture Will Be in 1988."[6] He sold over four million copies, and when the Rapture failed to occur, he simply cranked out a revised copy that was titled, "89 Reasons Why . . ." You know the rest.

And then there was Harold Camping who published a book in 1992 in which he predicted that the Rapture would occur on September 6, 1994.[7] He owned a nationwide radio network, so he was able to reach many people with his preposterous claim. Nor did he learn from his failure. He resurrected his prediction in 2011, pointing to May 21 as the "absolute date."[8] He plastered the nation with billboards. And when his prediction flopped again, he announced that he had "miscalculated," and that the Rapture would really take place in October!

A Prophetic Fulfillment

The ironic thing is that all this mockery of the Rapture is a fulfillment of end time prophecy. We are told in 2 Peter 3:

> 3) Know this first of all, that in the last days mockers will come with their mocking, following after their own lusts,

> 4) and saying, "Where is the promise of His coming? For ever since the fathers fell asleep, all continues just as it was from the beginning of creation."

A Satanic Conspiracy

Satan loves date setters. That's because their failed predictions cause Bible prophecy to be held in contempt, and that contempt extends to responsible teachers who are appalled by the sensational claims of their colleagues.

Satan does not want anyone studying end time Bible prophecy because the message of those prophecies is that we as Christians are going to win in the end. Bible prophecy clearly reveals the total defeat of Satan and the glorious triumph of Jesus.

Apathy in the Church

The extent to which prophecy is held in contempt within the Church today can be vividly demonstrated by an experience I'm aware of that occurred in 2011. That year, I was invited to be one of several speakers at a Bible prophecy conference hosted by Maranatha Evangelistic Ministries at a church in Broussard, Louisiana, which is a suburb of Lafayette.

The keynote speaker was the best known Bible prophecy teacher in America — namely, Tim LaHaye. The organizer of the conference, which was to be held on a Friday and Saturday, called all the largest Baptist churches in the Lafayette area and offered to provide them with Tim LaHaye, free of charge, as a Sunday morning preacher. All of them turned down the offer!

In addition to date setting, many pastors are wary of Bible prophecy because of all the sensationalism that has come to characterize it — and rightfully so. It seems that someone is always predicting an apocalyptic event due to blood moons or the alignment of the planets or the transition to a new century (remember all the hullabaloo over Y2K?). It's this kind of nonsense that often causes me to be embarrassed to reveal that I am a person who specializes in the teaching of Bible prophecy.

Again, Satan sits on the sidelines laughing.

The Crucial Question

So, what about the Rapture? Is it fact or fiction? Is it taught in the Bible or is it the product of over-active imaginations? Can it be justified with the Scriptures or is it just another case of sensationalism gone haywire?

Well, before I explain the Rapture and then proceed to prove that the concept is biblically based, I must first of all explain what happens when you die.[9] Unless you understand this, the Rapture will prove to be a confusing concept.

Death Before and After the Cross

Regarding death, the Bible teaches that before the death of Jesus on the cross, when people died, their spirits — whether saved or not — went to a holding place called Sheol in the Old Testament and Hades in the New Testament. Sheol is the Hebrew word; Hades is the Greek word.

This place was described by Jesus as having two compartments — one for the saved and the other for the unsaved (Luke 16:19-31). The compartment for the saved was called "Paradise" or "Abraham's Bosom." The compartment for the unsaved was named "Torments."

Hades is not the same place as Hell. This needs to be made clear because some translations confuse the two and translate Hades as Hell. Hades is a temporary holding place for the spirits of the dead. Hell is the eternal destination of those who are unsaved. They currently reside in Hades in the compartment called Torments.

The reason the spirits of the saved did not go directly to Heaven is because their faith only covered their sins, but did not provide forgiveness of them. And thus, they could not be ushered into the presence of a Holy God. They had to wait until a perfect man who did not deserve death was willing to die for their sins. That perfect man was, of course, Jesus of Nazareth who was God in the flesh.

The Bible says that when Jesus died, He descended into Hades and made a proclamation (1 Peter 3:18-19). We are not told what He said, but undoubtedly it must have been, "The blood has been shed!" Because of His sacrifice on the cross, the sins of the saved were now not only covered but were completely forgiven, making it possible for them to be ushered into the presence of God the Father.

And so, in Ephesians 4:8-10, we are told that when Jesus ascended to Heaven, He took a "host of captives" with Him. Paradise was moved from Hades to Heaven — something later confirmed by the Apostle Paul in 2 Corinthians 12:2-4. In this passage, Paul states that he was taken up into Heaven, which he identifies as Paradise.

The Intermediate Body

The Bible also teaches that after death, everyone receives what is often referred to as "an intermediate spirit body." The name comes from the fact that this after-death body is a transitional one between our current mortal body and the immortal body that we as believers will receive at the time of our resurrection.

The fact that such an intermediate spirit body exists can be easily demonstrated from the Scriptures.

- When King Saul wanted to know how he would fare in an upcoming battle, he went to a witch at Endor and asked her to call up Samuel from the dead so that he could consult with him. Evidently thinking that her familiar demon spirit would appear, the witch was astonished when Samuel appeared instead and proceeded to condemn Saul for trafficking in the occult (1 Samuel 28:7-19). Both she and Saul immediately recognized Samuel when he appeared.

- When Jesus told the story of Lazarus and the Rich Man, he made it clear that they fully recognized each other after they died and their spirits went to Hades, Lazarus to the compartment called Paradise, and the Rich Man to the compartment called Torments. Their spirits were incorporated into identifiable bodies (Luke 16:19-31).

- At His transfiguration, Jesus was joined by Moses and Elijah, and the apostles who were present were able to recognize both men as they talked with Jesus (Matthew 17:1-7).

- When the Apostle John was taken up to Heaven, he saw an immense multitude of people in white robes standing before the throne of God with palm branches in their hands. When he asked who they were, he was told that they were martyrs coming out of the Great Tribulation (Revelation 7:9-15).

In each of these cases, we see dead people whose spirits have been incorporated into recognizable bodies that are clothed.

A Summary

So, what happens when you die? If you are a child of God, your spirit is immediately ushered into the presence of Jesus by His holy angels. You are given an intermediate spirit body, and you remain in Heaven, in the presence of God, until the time of the Rapture.

A Definition

And so we come to the Rapture. Let's begin our consideration of this very important promise of God with a definition.

I would define the Rapture as an imminent blessing that is promised to Church Age believers. It is the promise that at any moment the living and dead in Christ will be snatched out of this world and taken to Heaven.

The event will be signaled by the shout of an archangel and the blowing of a trumpet. Jesus will appear in the heavens, bringing with Him the spirits of the dead in Christ.

Those believers who have died will have their bodies resurrected. Their spirits will be reunited with their bodies, and they will be instantly glorified, receiving immortality.

Those of us who are alive will follow, and on the way up to meet the Lord, we will be transformed from mortal to immortal, receiving our glorified bodies. We will then return to Heaven with Jesus.

Those left behind will have to face the terror of the Antichrist during seven years of unparalleled tribulation here on earth.

Do you see why this promise to the Church is described in the Scriptures as a blessing with which we are "to comfort one another"? (1Thessalonians 4:18).

At this point, you are probably thinking, "Okay, it is a great promise, but is it for real or is it just the product of fertile imaginations? Is there any scriptural basis for such a belief?"

The Rapture in Scripture

The answer is that the concept is not only in the Scriptures, but it can be found there in great detail. Here is the Apostle Paul's presentation of it in 1 Thessalonians 4:

> 13) But we do not want you to be uninformed, brethren, about those who are asleep, so that you will not grieve as do the rest who have no hope.

> 14) For if we believe that Jesus died and rose again, even so God will bring with Him those who have fallen asleep in Jesus.

> 15) For this we say to you by the word of the Lord, that we who are alive and remain until the coming of the Lord, will not precede those who have fallen asleep.

16) For the Lord Himself will descend from heaven with a shout, with the voice of the archangel and with the trumpet of God, and the dead in Christ will rise first.

17) Then we who are alive and remain will be caught up together with them in the clouds to meet the Lord in the air, and so we shall always be with the Lord.

18) Therefore comfort one another with these words.

Please note that in verse 15 Paul says this was a direct revelation to him from Jesus.

As you can readily see, this passage is very straight-forward and easy to understand. The only way to get around its plain sense meaning is to argue that it doesn't mean what it says, and then proceed to spiritualize it. This is exactly what many biblical commentators have done.

Most denominations deal with this passage by claiming that it is just another description of the Lord's Second Coming. But that cannot be true for some very obvious reasons.

There are only two detailed descriptions of the Lord's return in the New Testament — the one in 1 Thessalonians 4 and the other in Revelation 19.

There is no doubt that the one in Revelation is a description of the Second Coming. When you compare it to the description in 1 Thessalonians 4, a major problem emerges. The problem is that these two descriptions have nothing in common except that they both focus on Jesus. They are as different as night and day.

Consider the chart on the next page that shows how different they are.

1 Thessalonians 4	Revelation 19
Jesus appears in the heavens	Jesus returns to earth
Jesus appears **for** His Church	Jesus returns **with** His Church
Jesus appears as a Deliverer	Jesus returns as a Warrior
Jesus appears in Grace	Jesus returns in Wrath
Jesus appears as a Bridegroom	Jesus returns as King of kings

How can these two passages be describing the same event?

The distinction between the two becomes even clearer when the Rapture passage is compared to other descriptions of the Second Coming. Consider Jesus' brief description of the Second Coming contained in Matthew 24:27-31 —

- Whereas the Rapture is always pictured as an imminent event, Jesus says His Second Coming will occur following many signs that will point to the event.

- At the Rapture, Jesus gathers His saints, but at the Second Coming Jesus says that angels will gather them.

- And Jesus says in the Matthew passage that His return to earth will be heralded by supernatural phenomena in the heavens — the darkening of the sun and moon, and stars falling from the skies. Nothing like this is mentioned in the Rapture passage.

Another important distinction is mentioned in Matthew 24:37-38 where we are told that the Lord will come during a time of relative peace and prosperity, when the world is not expecting judgment from God. Yet, in chapter 19 of the book of Revelation the Lord is portrayed as returning to this earth at a time when the whole world is engulfed in war and chaos.

These verses cannot be speaking of the same event. The passage in Matthew 24:27-38 must be speaking of the Rapture, whereas Revelation 19 is talking about the Second Coming.

Another distinction can be found when comparing 1 Thessalonians 4:13-18 with Luke 17:34-37. In the Rapture passage in 1 Thessalonians 4, the redeemed are gathered and taken to Heaven. In the Luke passage, which speaks of the Second Coming, it is the unredeemed who are gathered and taken to where the vultures feed!

An Old Testament Comparison

The distinction between the Rapture and the Second Coming can also be demonstrated using a classic passage from the Hebrew Scriptures about the Lord's return to this earth. The passage is found in Zechariah 14:

> 1) Behold, a day is coming for the LORD when the spoil taken from you will be divided among you.
>
> 2) For I will gather all the nations against Jerusalem to battle, and the city will be captured, the houses plundered, the women ravished and half of the city exiled, but the rest of the people will not be cut off from the city.
>
> 3) Then the LORD will go forth and fight against those nations, as when He fights on a day of battle.
>
> 4) In that day His feet will stand on the Mount of Olives, which is in front of Jerusalem on the east; and the Mount of Olives will be split in its middle from east to west by a very large valley, so that half of the mountain will move toward

the north and the other half toward the south.

9) And the LORD will be king over all the earth; in that day the LORD will be the only one, and His name the only one.

Zechariah goes on in the following verses to say that Jesus will conquer all the armies with a supernatural word:

12) And this shall be the plague wherewith the LORD will smite all the people that have fought against Jerusalem; Their flesh shall consume away while they stand upon their feet, and their eyes shall consume away in their holes, and their tongue shall consume away in their mouth.

So, Zechariah says the Lord will return to the Mount of Olives, speak a supernatural word that will destroy all the armies gathered against Israel and Jerusalem, and will then begin to reign over all the earth.

Now, with this passage in mind, let's take a look at a description that Jesus gave about His return which is found in John 14:

1) "Do not let your heart be troubled; believe in God, believe also in Me.

2) "In My Father's house are many dwelling places; if it were not so, I would have told you; for I go to prepare a place for you.

3) "If I go and prepare a place for you, I will come again and receive you to Myself, that where I am, there you may be also."

As you can see, these two descriptions of the return of Jesus are as different as they can be. In the Zechariah account, Jesus comes to earth in wrath to reign. In the account in the Gospel of John, Jesus just appears in the heavens in grace to take believers back to Heaven with Him.

How can the differences be explained?

The difference is that Zechariah is speaking of the Second Coming, whereas Jesus in John 14 is speaking of the Rapture of the Church — two distinctly different events.

So, "What's it all about?"

Let's answer that question by taking a look at the most frequently asked questions about the Rapture, and in the process we will hopefully come to a clearer understanding of the reality, nature and importance of the Rapture.

11:59

A song by the Jeff Treece Band ©

Time is winding down.
Just look around us.
Evil's breaking loose on every side.
The devil knows his time is almost over,
But soon the clock will stop,
And Jesus Christ will split the sky.

Chorus:
So shout it from the rooftops,
Proclaim it in the streets.
Tell your friends and neighbors,
Tell everyone you meet:
"We all need a Savior,
But we're running out of time.
He's coming back at midnight,
And it's 11:59."

God's prepared a place for all His children
Free from fear and doubt, tears and pain.
But we must choose our destination.
There's just one way to Heaven,
And Jesus is His name.

At the right hand of the Father,
He'll soon stand to His feet
And hear: "Son go get My children,
And bring them home to Me."

He's coming for a Bride
That's spotless and pure,
Washed in the blood
And ready to go.
Time is running out;
It's almost midnight — it's 11:59.

Part 2

The Questions

1 What about the timing of the Rapture? When is it most likely to occur?

This is the most frequently asked question and the most controversial one. The reason it is so hotly debated is because the Bible does not specifically reveal the timing of the Rapture. All positions on the timing must be based on inferences, and thus there can be legitimate differences in opinion.

I personally believe the best inference of the Scriptures is that the Rapture will occur before the terrible seven year period of the Tribulation that is described in detail in the book of Revelation. In other words, I believe in what is called a Pre-Tribulation Rapture.

Let's take a look at those inferences.

(1) Deliverance from Wrath

The first derives from the fact that the Tribulation is a time of the pouring out of God's wrath, from beginning to end, and **Christians are promised immunity from the wrath of God**.

The Apostle Paul stresses this point in his first letter to the Thessalonians, in chapter 1, verse 10. He declares that believers are waiting ". . . for His Son from heaven, whom He raised from the dead, that is Jesus, *who rescues us from the wrath to come*" (emphasis added).

Paul makes a similar statement in 1 Thessalonians 5:9 where he emphasizes that "*God has not destined us for wrath*, but for obtaining salvation through our Lord Jesus Christ . . ." (emphasis added).

In like manner, in the letter that Jesus dictated to the church at Philadelphia, He promised that His Church would be kept from the time of Tribulation (Revelation 3:10):

> Because you have kept the word of My perseverance, I also will keep you from the hour of testing, that hour which is about to come upon the whole world, to test those who dwell on the earth.

(2) The Focus of the Tribulation

The next inference of a Pre-Tribulation Rapture is a very important one that is often overlooked. There is no purpose for the Church during the Tribulation because **the focus of this entire seven year period is the Jewish people**.

To understand this point, we must go back 2,500 years to the time of Daniel while he was in captivity in Babylon. He had read Jeremiah's prophecy that the captivity would last 70 years, and he realized that they were now in the 69th year of captivity, and the people had not repented.

So, he got on his knees and prayed for God to forgive him and his nation, asking the Lord to deliver them from captivity and to reconcile them to Him.

In response, God sent the Angel Gabriel to give him one of the most remarkable prophecies in the Bible — what is known as the Prophecy of the 70 Weeks of Years (a period of 490 years). During that time period, God promised that He was going to accomplish six things among the Jewish people:

1) "To finish the transgression" (by accepting the Messiah).

2) "To make an end of sin" (the repentance of a remnant).

3) "To make atonement for infirmity" (the Messiah to die for sins).

4) "To bring in everlasting righteousness" (the establishment of the Messiah's reign).

5) "To seal up vision and prophecy" (fulfill all Messianic prophecies).

6) "To anoint the most holy place" (provide a new temple).

Gabriel further told Daniel that from the time a decree was issued to rebuild Jerusalem, it would be 483 years until the coming of the Messiah, who would be killed. Shortly thereafter Jerusalem would be destroyed. The final seven years of the prophecy would begin when the Antichrist makes a covenant with Israel (Daniel 9:27).

Just as was prophesied, it was 483 years from the time that Artaxerxes issued an edict for the Jews to rebuild Jerusalem to the time when Jesus was crucified. And shortly thereafter, just as prophesied, Jerusalem and the temple were destroyed by the Romans in 70 AD.

When Jesus was crucified, the clock stopped ticking on the 490 years of Daniel's prophecy because God placed the Jewish people under discipline due to their rejection of Jesus as their Messiah. They were scattered throughout the world.

We know for certain that there is a gap in the fulfillment of Daniel's prophecy because during the 483 year period, only one of the six goals of the Lord was accomplished — namely, number 3, the atonement for sins. The other five goals will be accomplished during the last week of years of Daniel's prophecy.

Those seven years are what we refer to as the Tribulation

when God will pour out His wrath on a pagan world and the rebellious Jewish people.

Those last seven years are referred to in the Hebrew Scriptures as:

- "The time of Jacob's distress" — Jeremiah 30:7.

- "A time of distress such as has never occurred" — Daniel 12:1.

- "The hour of testing . . . to come upon the whole world" — Revelation 3:10.

- Jesus also called it a time of "great tribulation" — Matthew 24:21.

- And He used the same terminology in Revelation 7:14 — "the great tribulation."

The Church Age began with an overlap period during which God began to focus on the Church while still working among the Jewish people. The Church was established around 30 AD, but the Jews were not set aside in discipline until 40 years later in 70 AD, when the Romans destroyed Jerusalem and the Temple.

In like manner, I believe we are now in another overlap period of time that began with the re-establishment of Israel in 1948. While the Church continues, God has started working among the Jewish people once again, regathering them from the four corners of the earth and re-establishing their nation-state.

The Church will soon be taken out of this world before God once again gives His undivided attention to the Jewish people during the 70th week of Daniel's 70 Weeks of Years.

Again, there is just no purpose for the Church here on earth during the Tribulation. The Tribulation is when God's focus returns to Israel.

(3) The Emphasis on Imminency

This brings us to another very important inference, one that many prophecy experts consider to be the most important. Only the Pre-Tribulation view of the Rapture allows for imminence.

We are told over and over in the New Testament that the Lord's return is imminent and that we should live looking for it to occur any moment. Take, for example, Matthew 24:

> 36) "But of that day and hour no one knows, not even the angels of heaven, nor the Son, but the Father alone.
>
> 42) "Therefore be on the alert, for you do not know which day your Lord is coming.
>
> 44) "For this reason you also must be ready; for the Son of Man is coming at an hour when you do not think He will."

Jesus repeated this warning in Matthew 25, in His parable of the ten virgins. He declared that believers should live with an eternal perspective, expecting the Lord to return at any moment. He concluded the parable with these words: "Be on the alert then, for you do not know the day nor the hour" (Matthew 25:13).

Likewise, Luke in his gospel quotes Jesus as telling His disciples to "keep alert at all times," for the Lord's return, implying it could occur at any moment (Luke 21:36).

There are many other imminence passages in the New Testament. Listed below are some examples. In each case, I have added emphasis to key words.

> ***You too, be ready***; for the Son of Man is coming at an hour that you do not expect (Luke 12:40).

Do this, knowing the time, that it is already the hour for you to awaken from sleep; for now *salvation is nearer to us than when we believed. The night is almost gone, and the day is near.* Therefore let us lay aside the deeds of darkness and put on the armor of light (Romans 13:11-12).

. . . you are not lacking in any gift, *awaiting eagerly the revelation of our Lord Jesus Christ* . . . (1 Corinthians 1:7).

If anyone does not love the Lord, he is to be accursed. *Maranatha!* (1 Corinthians 16:22). [Aramaic for "Oh, Lord come!"]

For our citizenship is in heaven, from which also *we eagerly wait for a Savior*, the Lord Jesus Christ (Philippians 3:20).

Let your gentle spirit be known to all men. *The Lord is near* (Philippians 4:5).

[We are to live] *looking for the blessed hope* and the appearing of the glory of our great God and Savior, Christ Jesus (Titus 2:13).

You too be patient; strengthen your hearts, *for the coming of the Lord is near.* Do not complain, brethren, against one another, so that you yourselves may not be judged; behold, *the Judge is standing right at the door* (James 5:8-9).

Therefore, *prepare your minds for action*, keep sober in spirit, fix your hope completely on the grace to be brought to you at the revelation of Jesus Christ (1 Peter 1:13).

> *The end of all things is near*; therefore, be of sound judgment and sober spirit for the purpose of prayer (1 Peter 4:7).

> [Jesus speaking] Behold, *I am coming quickly*. Blessed is he who heeds the words of the prophecy of this book (Revelation 22:7-12).

As you can readily see from these verses we are exhorted to live with an eternal perspective, expecting the Lord to come any moment.

These verses must be talking about the Rapture and not the Second Coming for two reasons.

First, the Second Coming is not an imminent event because there are too many prophecies that must be fulfilled before Jesus can return to this earth. For example:

- There must be Seven years of Tribulation.

- A Temple must be rebuilt in Jerusalem.

- The Antichrist must be revealed.

- The Two Witnesses in Jerusalem must be killed.

- The rebuilt Temple in Jerusalem must be desecrated.

- The Mark of the Beast must be instituted.

- A Jewish remnant must repent and be saved.

The point again: The only way the Lord's return can be imminent is for there to be a Rapture that is separate and apart from the Second Coming and which can occur at any moment, without the fulfillment of any prophecies.

The second reason the imminence warnings must refer to the Rapture and not the Second Coming is because the date of the Second Coming can be precisely calculated. That's because the book of Revelation reveals that the Second Coming will occur exactly 2,520 days after the Tribulation begins (Revelation 11:3 and 12:6).

(4) Biblical Examples

This brings us to a fourth inference of a Pre-Tribulation Rapture. Based on biblical examples, God always removes His elect before He pours out His judgmental, apocalyptic wrath (as opposed to His remedial judgments).

Thus, the Apostle Peter says that if God spared Noah and his family from the flood, then He "knows how to rescue the godly from tribulation, and to keep the unrighteous under punishment for the day of judgment" (2 Peter 2:4-9).

Enoch, a Gentile, who I believe was symbolic of the Church, was taken out of the world before the flood, whereas Noah and his family, symbolic of the Jews, were preserved through the flood (Genesis 5:21-24).

Another example is the removal of Lot and his family from Sodom & Gomorrah before the cities were destroyed (Genesis 19:1-26). Lot was even told to speed up his escape because the Lord could not destroy the cites until he left (verse 22).

And then there is Rahab, the harlot in Jericho, who provided refuge for the Jewish spies who were sent to scout out the city. She protected them because she expressed to them her faith in their God (Joshua 2:9-11).

We are told in Joshua 6:22-23 that God arranged for her and all her family to be removed from the city before it was conquered by Joshua and his army.

I believe these examples make it clear why we are never told to watch for the Antichrist. Rather, we are told to watch for Jesus Christ.

2 **Is the Rapture mentioned in the book of Revelation, and, if so, where?**

It is not specifically mentioned, but it is definitely inferred.[10] And the place where it is inferred points to a Pre-Trib Rapture.

The book of Revelation focuses on the Church in the first three chapters. In fact, chapters 2 and 3 contain seven letters that Jesus dictated to seven churches located in modern day Turkey.

But then, at the beginning of chapter 4, a door is opened in Heaven, and the Apostle John is caught up to the throne room of God where he is shown a preview of the Great Tribulation.

After chapter 4, there is no more mention of the Church in the book of Revelation until chapter 22, verse 16 — after the Tribulation has ended.

There is mention of "saints," but these would be those who are saved during the Tribulation in response to the Rapture, the Word of God (Bibles people will find), the wrath of God (Isaiah 26:9), the evangelism of 144,000 Jews (Revelation 7), the preaching of the Two Witnesses in Jerusalem (Revelation 11) and the proclamation of the Gospel by an angel who circumnavigates the globe at the end of the Tribulation, right before the final pouring out of God's wrath (Revelation 14:6-7).

Thus, the rapture of John in chapter 4 appears to be a symbolic type of the Rapture of the Church.

This symbolism of the Church in Heaven is reinforced by the fact that when John gets to Heaven, he sees 24 elders sitting around God's throne with golden crowns on their heads (Revelation 4:4). They were singing a song praising Jesus for having redeemed them with His blood — as well as "men from every tribe and tongue and people and nation" (Revelation 5:9). This would definitely seem to be an acknowledgment that the 24 elders represent those saved during the Church Age.

Further, a Pre-Trib Rapture of the Church is implied in chapter 19 of Revelation, where the Bride of Christ (the Church) is pictured celebrating its union with its Bridegroom (Jesus) at the Marriage Feast of the Lamb (verse 7). This takes place at the end of the Tribulation on earth. When the feast is concluded, Jesus returns to earth in His Second Coming, and He brings His Bride with Him.

3 Is there any mention of the Rapture in Jesus' Olivet Discourse (Matthew 24) about the end times?

Many very fine Bible prophecy experts have taken the position that the Rapture is nowhere to be found in the Olivet Discourse. They argue that the Lord's entire presentation in Matthew 24 is about the Second Coming. But I respectfully disagree with that position.

I believe Jesus shifts His focus from the Second Coming to the Rapture at verse 36 and continues talking about it through verse 44. The first reason I see the Rapture in these verses is because Jesus says, "of that day and hour no one knows." How could He possibly be referring to His Second Coming? Keep in mind that He has just told His disciples exactly when He was going to return — "immediately after the tribulation of those days" (Matthew 24:29).

From both the prophecies of Daniel and the book of Revelation, we know the Tribulation will last exactly 7 prophetic years (years of 360 days each). Anyone living at the beginning of the Tribulation (when the Antichrist signs a treaty with Israel) could calculate the exact day of the Lord's return because we are told that the Tribulation will last precisely 2,520 days (Revelation 11:3 and Revelation 12:6).

So, again, when Jesus says no one can know the day of His return, He must be speaking of the Rapture, and not the Second Coming.

Next, Jesus says that when He returns, society will be like it was in the days of Noah, when right up to the last moment people were "eating and drinking" and "marrying and giving in marriage" (Matthew 24:38). In other words, life will be continuing as normal when He returns.

But this could not be talking about the Second Coming because life will be anything but normal at the end of the Tribulation. At that time more than half the population of the world will have been killed, including two-thirds of the Jews. The whole world, according to what we are told in Revelation 13-19, will be in absolute chaos.

Additionally, if you will take a look at the Olivet Discourse as it is recorded in Luke 21, you will find that Luke adds an observation that Matthew's account does not contain. In the section where Jesus starts talking about how His return could occur any moment, Luke quotes Him as saying: "Watch therefore, and pray always that you may be counted worthy to escape all these things that will come to pass, and to stand before the Son of Man" (Luke 21:36, NKJV).

Those words sure sound to me like a reference to the Rapture of the Church.

4 **Some argue that the Rapture is most likely to occur in the middle of the Tribulation or near the end. What is wrong with these viewpoints concerning the timing?**

There are two fundamental problems with placing the Rapture in the middle or near the end of the Tribulation.

The first is that both of these timings for the Rapture subject the Church to the wrath of God. Those who propose a mid-Trib Rapture or a late-Trib Rapture always argue that either the Seal Judgments, or both the Seal and the Trumpet Judgments, represent the wrath of Man and Satan, and not the wrath of God. They thus end up arguing that only the Bowl Judgments, portrayed in Revelation 16, constitute the wrath of God.

But this argument cannot be sustained. The Seal Judgments in Revelation 6 are portrayed as coming directly from the throne of God (Revelation 6:1). Furthermore, it is stated point-blank in Revelation 6:16 that the Seal Judgments are "the wrath of the Lamb," referring to Jesus.

The opening of the seventh seal leads right into the Trumpet Judgments in chapter 8 of Revelation. And those judgments are pictured as coming from seven angels "who stand before God" (Revelation 8:2).

When the Bowl Judgments are introduced in Revelation 15, they are referred to as the last of the judgments "because in them the wrath of God is finished" (Revelation 15:1). So, the Bowl Judgments are not the beginning of God's wrath. Rather, they are the completion of His wrath.

The book of Revelation makes it clear that the wrath that is poured out on the earth during those terrible seven years is the wrath of God, from beginning to the end. And, as I have pointed out before, the Bible promises that believers will be delivered from God's wrath.

The second problem with placing the Rapture in the middle of the Tribulation or near the end is that such timing destroys imminency.

If the Seal Judgments or both the Seal and Trumpet Judgments must take place before the Rapture can occur, then the Rapture is not imminent, and believers should be living looking for the Antichrist and not Jesus Christ.

5 Could the Rapture occur at the end of the Tribulation as a stage in the Second Coming of the Lord?

This is what is often referred to derisively as the "Yo-Yo Rapture" because it pictures believers being taken up into the heavens to meet the Lord and then immediately returning to earth with Him.

Again, this concept subjects the Church to the full seven years of God's wrath during the Tribulation. It also destroys imminency.

The Rapture is pictured in the Scriptures as the Bridegroom (Jesus) coming for His Bride (the Church). This Post-Trib view of the Rapture presents a warped concept of the Bridegroom beating up His Bride for seven years, and then coming for her!

At one of our annual Bible conferences, the great Bible teacher, Ron Rhodes, addressed this Post-Trib concept of the Rapture in this way:[11]

> Let's imagine for a moment that Post-Tribulationism is true. Here's what this view of the Rapture is saying:
>
> - You will go through the seven years of God's wrath.
> - You will suffer through the terrible reign of the Antichrist.
> - You will experience the agonizing Seal, Trumpet and Bowl Judgments — which will grow progressively worse and increasingly painful.
> - Most of you will die painful deaths as martyrs.
>
> "Therefore, encourage one another with these words" (1 Thessalonians 4:18).

I'm sorry, friends — it just doesn't work!

There is another very serious problem with the Post-Tribulation viewpoint: it does not provide a population for the Millennium! Let me explain.

The Bible teaches that at the Second Coming, Jesus is going to judge all the people left alive at that point in time — at the end of the Tribulation (Matthew 25:31-46 and Ezekiel 20:33-38). The saved will enter the Millennium in the flesh and will begin to repopulate the world. The saved who were raptured at the beginning of the Tribulation will be scattered around the world to reign with Jesus in their glorified bodies.

All those who have resisted the Lord to the end of the Tribulation will be consigned to death.

Now, if the Rapture occurs at the same time as the Second Coming, as part of the Second Coming, there will be no one to enter the Millennium in the flesh! All the saved will have received glorified bodies in the Rapture, and all the unsaved will have been consigned to Hades.

The only way to have a Millennial population in the flesh is for the Rapture to occur at a time earlier than and separate from the Second Coming.

6 Is 1 Thessalonians 4 the only Rapture passage contained in the New Testament?

Not at all.

Jesus referred to the Rapture in John 14 when He said:

1) "Do not let your heart be troubled; believe in God, believe also in Me.

2) "In My Father's house are many dwelling places; if it were not so, I would have told you; for I go to prepare a place for you.

3) "If I go and prepare a place for you, I will come again and receive you to Myself, that where I am, there you may be also.

4) "And you know the way where I am going."

How do we know Jesus is speaking here of the Rapture? Because He says He will take believers to Heaven. If He were talking about the Second Coming, He would focus on believers reigning with Him here on the earth.

Another Rapture passage can be found in 1 Corinthians 15. The Apostle Paul talks about the Rapture when he reveals what he calls a "mystery" (verse 51). He asserts that "we shall not all sleep [a biblical euphemism for death], but we shall all be changed" (verse 51). What he is saying here is that not all of us are going to die, but all believers are going to be changed from mortal to immortal.

This is exactly what is taught in 1 Thessalonians 4:13-18. Those who are dead in Christ will be resurrected and glorified. Living believers will not taste death. They will be caught up to meet Jesus in the sky, and on the way up, "this mortal will put on immortality" (1 Corinthians 15:53).

In his letter to Titus, Paul exhorted him (and us) to live "looking for the blessed hope and the appearing of the glory of our great God and Savior, Christ Jesus" (Titus 2:13). Notice, this verse refers to the Lord's "appearing" and not to His coming to earth. It also makes no reference to judgment, which will occur at the Second Coming.

In 2 Thessalonians chapter 2, Paul says that the appearance of the Antichrist is being restrained and that "the lawless one" will not be revealed until the restrainer "is taken out of the way" (verses 6-8). So, there is a restrainer of evil that must be removed from the world before the Tribulation can begin. Who is that restrainer? Who else could it be but the

Holy Spirit working through the Church? When the Church is removed in the Rapture, the Antichrist will appear on the scene and evil will explode all across the world.

In that same chapter — 2 Thessalonians 2 — I believe Paul presents another statement concerning the Rapture that also indicates that the Rapture will occur before the Tribulation begins. It is found in verse 3 where he states: "Let no one in any way deceive you, for it ["the day of the Lord" in verse 2] will not come unless the apostasy comes first, and the man of lawlessness is revealed, the son of destruction."

In this verse Paul is saying that "the day of the Lord," which is the period of the Tribulation and the Millennium, will not come until "the apostasy comes first." What does this have to do with a Pre-Trib Rapture? It is the fact that the word, apostasy, is an interpretation and not a translation.

The actual Greek word used in this verse means "departure." Tommy Ice, the director of the Pre-Trib Study Center, has pointed out that the first seven English translations of the Bible all translated the word as "departure." They were as follows:[12]

1) The Wycliffe Bible   (1384)
2) The Tyndale Bible   (1526)
3) The Coverdale Bible   (1535)
4) The Cranmer Bible   (1539)
5) The Great Bible   (1540)
6) The Beeches Bible   (1576)
7) The Geneva Bible   (1608)

Further, the Bible used by the Western world from 400 AD to the 1600s — Jerome's Latin translation known as "The Vulgate" — rendered the Greek word with a Latin word, which meant "departure."

The first translation of the word to mean apostasy in an English Bible did not occur until 1611 when the King James

Version was issued. So, why did the King James translators introduce a completely new rendering of the word as "falling away," to indicate apostasy? The best guess is that they were taking a stab at the false teachings of Catholicism.

Another indication that Paul is talking about the departure of the Church from this world, and not a departure of the Church from doctrinal orthodoxy, is the fact that a definite article is used with the Greek word, rendering it "*the* departure."

This indicates that Paul was pointing to a particular type of departure that the Thessalonian church was familiar with — namely, the Rapture.

7 Is there any mention of the Rapture in the Old Testament?

Not specifically, which is the reason that Paul referred to the Rapture in 1 Corinthians 15:51 as a "mystery," meaning it was something not clearly revealed in the Hebrew Scriptures.

The reason the Rapture was not revealed in the Old Testament is because it is a promise to Church Age saints and not to those believers who lived before the establishment of the Church. Believers who lived in Old Testament times — both Jews and Gentiles — will be resurrected at the end of the Tribulation when Jesus returns to this earth in the Second Coming (Daniel 12:1-2).

But, as prophecy scholar Jim Tetlow has pointed out, the Hebrew Scriptures contain "shadows" of the Rapture.[13] He refers to Romans 15:4, which says, "For whatever was written in earlier times [in the Old Testament] was written for our instruction, so that through perseverance and the encouragement of the Scriptures we might have hope." He then adds: "Though the Rapture was hidden in part from Old Testament believers, the symbolic types found throughout foreshadow a future Rapture when God will remove His people prior to pouring out His wrath on a Christ-rejecting world."

Accordingly, symbolic types of the Rapture can be found throughout the Hebrew Scriptures. For example, as I have pointed out before, Enoch, a Gentile symbolic of the Church, was taken out of the world before the Noahic Flood, while Noah and his family, representative of the Jewish remnant, were left on earth but were protected through the calamity.

And again, the Rapture principle can also be found in the story of Lot and his family, all of whom were delivered from Sodom and Gomorrah before the cities were destroyed by God.

The Apostle Peter referred to these examples in chapter 2 of his second epistle:

> 5) [For if God] did not spare the ancient world, but preserved Noah, a preacher of righteousness, with seven others, when He brought a flood upon the world of the un-godly;
>
> 6) and if He condemned the cities of Sodom and Gomorrah to destruction . . .
>
> 7) [but] rescued righteous Lot . . .
>
> 9) then the Lord knows how to rescue the godly from temptation, and to keep the un-righteous under punishment for the day of judgment . . .

Tetlow proceeds to provide several other symbolic ex-amples of the Rapture principle, but he also singles out two passages of scripture that present a possible picture of a Rapture preceding the Tribulation. The first is found in Isaiah 26:

> 20) Come, my people, enter into your rooms

and close your doors behind you; hide for a
little while until indignation runs its course.

21) For behold, the LORD is about to come out
from His place to punish the inhabitants of the
earth for their iniquity . . .

The second is a passage that is found in the writings of the
Minor Prophets — in Zephaniah 2:

2) . . . before the day of the LORD's anger comes upon
you.

3) Seek the LORD, all you humble of the earth who
have carried out His ordinances; seek righteousness,
seek humility. Perhaps you will be hidden in the day
of the LORD's anger.

These two passages are probably more relevant to the fact
that during the Tribulation, God is going to hide a Jewish
remnant in Edom, most likely in Petra (Daniel 11:41 and
Revelation 12:13-14). But they do demonstrate the Rapture
principle of protecting believers from the wrath of God.

Perhaps a better illustration of the Rapture principle is
found in Isaiah 57:1-2, which reads as follows: "The righteous perish, and no one takes it to heart; the devout are taken
away, and no one understands that the righteous are taken
away to be spared from evil" (NIV).

**8 If the Rapture is going to occur before the beginning
of the Tribulation, does that mean that there are going
to be two Second Comings of the Lord?**

No, it means the Second Coming is going to occur in two
stages — first, the Rapture before the Tribulation and then the
Return of the Lord at the end of the Tribulation.

It reminds me of a similar situation in the Old Testament.
The Hebrew prophets, when speaking of the Messiah to

come, painted two different pictures of Him. In some passages He was presented as a Suffering Lamb (Isaiah 53:2-10). But in others He was portrayed as a Conquering Lion (Jeremiah 25:30-31).

To reconcile these conflicting images, the Jewish sages concluded that there would be two Messiahs. One would be Messiah ben Joseph (the pastoral one). The other would be Messiah ben David (the warrior one).

But they were wrong. The passages were not speaking of two Messiahs. Rather, they were foretelling that the Messiah would come twice, first as the Suffering Lamb to die for the sins of Mankind, and then, subsequently, as the Conquering Lion to rule the world in majesty and glory.

Thus, just as the coming of the Lord in Old Testament prophecy was portrayed in two stages, in like manner, the return of the Lord in New Testament prophecy is pictured to occur in two stages.

9 What about Old Testament saints? Will they be included in the Rapture?

No. The Rapture is a promise to the Church. Only those who put their faith in Jesus during the Church Age, both the living and the dead, will be included in the Rapture.

Old Testament saints will be resurrected at the end of the Tribulation and will receive their glorified bodies at that time. This is clearly taught in Daniel chapter 12 where we are told that their resurrection will occur after the "time of distress such as has never occurred since there was a nation until that time . . ." (Daniel 12:1).

The Tribulation martyrs will also be resurrected at the same time as the Old Testament saints, at the end of the Tribulation. Both groups will receive their glorified bodies at that time.

10 You keep talking about Church Age believers receiving glorified bodies at the time of the Rapture. What is a glorified body?

This is a difficult question to answer with certainty. Paul devotes 24 verses to this topic in 1 Corinthians 15:35-58. He clarifies some things, but not everything.[14]

He states it will be an "imperishable body" that will be raised in "glory" and "power" (verse 43). He also states it will be a "spiritual body" (verse 46), but we know this does not mean it will be immaterial in nature because spirits do not have bodies, and we are told in Philippians 3:21 that our glorified body will be a body like the one that Jesus had after His resurrection.

When Jesus appeared to His disciples after His resurrection, His glorified body was tangible and recognizable (Luke 24:36-39). He also engaged in meals with His disciples (Luke 24:41-43 and John 21:9-13). But His glorified body had a different dimension to it because He could appear and disappear at will. He also seemed to move about at high speed, being in Jerusalem one moment and then appearing a short time later in the Galilee (John 21:1-7).

So, our glorified bodies will be similar to the ones we have now, but also different. They will be imperishable, glorious, powerful, and spiritual — but not in the sense of being a spirit. Rather, they will most likely be "spiritual" in the sense that they will be completely subjected to the guidance of the Holy Spirit.

And when Paul speaks of our glorified bodies being powerful, he is most likely referring to the fact, that like the resurrected body of Jesus, they will have a different dimension to them, allowing us to do things that are not possible in our present bodies — like appear and disappear and move about at high speed. This idea is implied in Philippians 3:21

where Paul wrote that when we are resurrected, Jesus "will transform the body of our humble state into conformity with the body of His glory, by the exertion of the power that He has even to subject all things to Himself."

Most important to me is the fact that Paul emphasizes that our current perishable bodies will become "imperishable" (1 Corinthians 15:53-54). As such, our bodies will no longer be subject to disease and pain and death.

Our glorified bodies will also be perfected. We are told in Isaiah 35:5-6 that "the eyes of the blind will be opened and the ears of the deaf will be unstopped." Further, "the lame will leap like a deer, and the tongue of the dumb will shout for joy."

Scripture passages like these help us to get a glimpse of the meaning of Paul's statement in the book of Romans where he wrote: "For I consider that the sufferings of this present time are not worthy to be compared with the glory that is to be revealed to us" (Romans 8:18).

11 Will those left behind at the time of the Rapture be given an opportunity to be saved?

Definitely.

The book of Revelation says that the vast majority of those left behind will refuse to repent and will, in fact, worship demons and money as well as idols made of wood and stone (Revelation 9:20-21). But, the book also reveals that there will be many who will repent and turn to God for salvation — "a great multitude which no one could count" (Revelation 7:9).

How can these people be saved if the Church is gone? The answer is that they will be saved by the power of the Holy Spirit who will still be in the world, drawing people to Jesus.

Keep in mind that the members of the Lord's Church have

a special indwelling of the Holy Spirit, and through that indwelling, the Holy Spirit restrains evil in the world. When the Church is removed in the Rapture, the Holy Spirit will not be removed because the Holy Spirit is omnipresent. He will continue His work of drawing people to Jesus, and He will accomplish this in several ways:

- Through the testimony of the Rapture.

- Through Bibles that people find.

- Through testimonies of the Gospel that people will find on the Internet before they can be erased.

- Through the testimony of the Two Witnesses who will be preaching daily in Jerusalem (Revelation 11).

- Through the witnessing of 144,000 Jews who will be sealed by the Spirit and protected by God throughout the Tribulation (Revelation 11).

- Through the proclamation of the Gospel to the whole world by an angel near the end of the Tribulation (Revelation 14:6).

The glorious truth that emerges from this mass salvation is that even when God pours out His wrath, His fundamental purpose is not to punish. Instead, his most passionate purpose is to bring people to repentance so that they might be saved. Here's how the prophet Isaiah put it: ". . . when the earth experiences Your judgments, the inhabitants of the world learn righteousness" (Isaiah 26:9).

There is a major point of controversy with regard to salvation after the Rapture. It concerns those who heard the Gospel before the Rapture and refused to accept it. Some argue that they will be ineligible to receive the Gospel and will thus continue to reject it. Others argue that they will be able to be saved.

The controversy is rooted in 2 Thessalonians 2:8-12,

which reads as follows:

> 8) Then that lawless one [the Antichrist] will be revealed whom the Lord will slay with the breath of His mouth and bring to an end by the appearance of His coming;
>
> 9) that is, the one whose coming is in accord with the activity of Satan, with all power and signs and false wonders,
>
> 10) and with all the deception of wickedness for those who perish, because they did not receive the love of the truth so as to be saved.
>
> 11) For this reason God will send upon them a deluding influence so that they will believe what is false,
>
> 12) in order that they all may be judged who did not believe the truth, but took pleasure in wickedness.

This passage seems to teach that people who have rejected the Gospel before the Rapture will continue to do so. Because of this passage, I cannot say with absolute confidence that those who have rejected the Gospel before the Rapture will have the possibility of accepting it afterwards. I hope those who argue that these people will be given another opportunity are correct, but I would not want to give such people any false hope.

One thing to keep in mind is that people who accept Jesus as their Lord and Savior during the Tribulation are going to be subjected to instant persecution and even martyrdom. Therefore, I find it highly unlikely that people who rejected the Gospel before the Tribulation will be willing to receive it once they find themselves in the midst of unparalleled persecution by the Antichrist.

12 Could there be a partial Rapture, consisting only of those Christians who are living godly lives and are watching for the Lord's appearance?

No, this is not a possibility.

The passages that describe the Rapture apply to all true Christians, whether mature in the faith or immature, and whether faithful or disobedient. Again, believers are promised deliverance from the wrath of God. And God is not going to create the Church on the basis of grace through faith and then divide it on the basis of works.

Those who argue for a partial Rapture base their case on Jesus' parable of the ten virgins (Matthew 25:1-13). In this parable, five of the virgins were ready for the Lord's return and were taken, while five who were not ready were left behind. Those who were left behind are not symbolic of unprepared believers. They had no oil (symbolic of the Holy Spirit) in their lamps. Proof positive of this is the fact that Jesus says to those left behind, "Truly I say to you, I do not know you" (verse 12).

Keep in mind also what is said in 1 John 2:28 — "Now, little children, abide in Him, so that when He appears, we may have confidence and not shrink away from Him in shame at His coming." This verse clearly indicates that some Christians taken in the Rapture will suffer shame. So, not just those living godly lives are going to be taken.

This conclusion is reinforced by 1 Corinthians 3:10-15 where the Apostle Paul explains that some who are taken in the Rapture will suffer shame when they stand before the judgment seat of Jesus and are judged as to how they used their spiritual gifts to advance the Lord's kingdom. They will be granted eternal life because of their faith in Jesus, but they will receive none of the special rewards that are promised to those believers who faithfully served the Lord. In fact, Paul indicates that all their useless works will be burned away, and they will be saved with their tail feathers smoking!

Jack Van Impe has pointed to another problem with the partial Rapture concept that is very insightful. He reminds us that the Bible states that every believer is a member of the body of Christ (Romans 12:4-5). He then observes: "Should only those who meet a certain standard of spirituality be taken, the body of Jesus Christ would be dismembered and disfigured."[15] He then adds, "The partial Rapture view, by definition, denies the teaching on the unity of our Lords' body."[16]

The only "Christians" who will be left behind will be those who profess to be Christian but have never been born again — people I refer to as "Cultural Christians."

13 Will all babies and minor children be taken to Heaven when the Rapture occurs?

This is a tough question to answer definitively, and that's because the Bible does not directly address the question. We can only work with inferences and logic.

The answers usually given in response to this question fall into two camps. The first is the position that all minor children will be taken in the Rapture. (Some even apply this to babies in the womb.) The other camp argues that only the minor children of believers will be taken.

Those who argue in behalf of all children being included in the Rapture usually present three strong arguments for their position.

First, they point to the attitude of Jesus toward children that is revealed in Mark 10 when He said:

14) ". . . Permit the children to come to Me; do not hinder them; for the kingdom of God belongs to such as these.

15) "Truly I say to you, whoever does not receive the kingdom of God like a child will not enter it at all."

Jesus also said in Matthew 18:3, "I tell you the truth, unless you change and become like little children, you will never enter the kingdom of heaven."

The second argument of those who are all-inclusive of children in the Rapture is based on what happened to the child that was born of the adultery between King David and Bathsheba (2 Samuel 12). During Bathsheba's pregnancy, the prophet Nathan confronted David with his sin and then told him that the death of the child would be his punishment.

When the prophecy came true, David consoled himself in his grief by saying, "I will go to him, but he will not return to me" (2 Samuel 12:23). Thus, the Holy Spirit revealed through David that when a minor child dies, its spirit goes to be with the Lord.

The third point made by the all-inclusive group is related to the age of accountability. They point out that although children are born with a sin nature due to the original sin of Adam, they are not responsible for Adam's sin, nor are they responsible for their own sins until they reach the age of accountability — the age at which they are able to discern between good and evil. Therefore, if a child dies before reaching the age of accountability, they will be saved.

These are powerful arguments in behalf of all minor children being included in the Rapture.

But they ignore a biblical reality. There is not one example in the Bible of minor children being spared from the wrath of God. Consider:

- When God poured out His wrath on Noah's generation with a worldwide flood, all of humanity died except Noah and his family.

- When God subjected the Egyptian people to His wrath by killing the firstborn of each family, none were spared, regardless of age. And this applied also to the firstborn of any Jewish family that refused to paint their door posts with the blood of an animal sacrifice.

- When God allowed Israel to be conquered by Assyria and Judah by the Babylonians, children were included in the massacres.

- When God poured out His wrath on the Jewish people in 70 AD through the Roman armies, children were not spared.

- And when God delivers His wrath during the Tribulation, resulting in half the population of the world being destroyed in the first three and a half years, there is no mention of children being protected.

Those who are all-inclusive of children in the Rapture respond by pointing to the deliverance of Noah and all his family. They also emphasize that Lot and all of his family were delivered from the destruction of Sodom and Gomorrah. But none of the children of Noah and Lot were minors. They were adult believers.

Those who argue that only the minor children of believers will be taken in the Rapture, normally point to the following two scripture passages:

> For the unbelieving husband is sanctified through his wife, and the unbelieving wife is sanctified through her believing husband; for otherwise your children are unclean, but now they are holy (1 Corinthians 7:14).

> In the fear of the LORD there is strong confidence, and his children will have refuge. (Proverbs 14:26).

The first of these passages is rather nebulous in its meaning. Here is how it is put in paraphrases designed to render its intent:

> For the unbelieving husband is, in a sense, consecrated by being joined to the person of his wife; the unbelieving wife is similarly consecrated by the Christian brother she has married. If this were not so then your children would bear the stains of paganism, whereas they are actually consecrated to God *(The Phillips New Testament)*.[17]

> For the believing wife brings holiness to her marriage, and the believing husband brings holiness to his marriage. Otherwise, your children would not be holy, but now they are holy *(The New Living Translation)*.[18]

Regardless of the translation or paraphrase, the sense of the passage seems to be that the minor children of even one believing parent are set apart to God as holy.

Well, I think you can see now why I said at the beginning that this is a very difficult question to answer.

Personally, I believe there are three fundamental truths that emerge from the Scriptures we have considered:

1) That children who die before the age of accountability go to Heaven.

2) That when God pours out His wrath, He does not spare children in general.

3) That God does provide special protection from His wrath for the children of believers.

Based on these truths, I have concluded that the only minor children who will be taken in the Rapture will be those who have at least one believing parent. I think it is also logical to conclude that when God takes Christians in the Rapture, He will not leave their minor children behind as orphans to face the terrors of the Antichrist.

14 **Couldn't God just protect believers during the Tribulation? Is it really necessary to remove them from the earth?**

Yes, the Lord could provide believers with supernatural protection. In fact, He will do precisely that when He provides saints who are converted during the Tribulation with protection from the stings of the demonic locust attack that will be part of the Trumpet Judgments (Revelation 9:4).

But God's promise to the Church during the Tribulation is not one of protection, but one of deliverance. Jesus said that when the signs pointing to the Tribulation "*begin* to take place," believers are to look up because their "redemption is drawing near" (Luke 21:28 – emphasis added). He also urged believers to pray that they might "escape all these things" (Luke 21:36).

There really is no purpose for the Church to be present during the Tribulation. It is a time of the pouring out of God's wrath upon those who have rejected His grace, love and mercy.

Again, there are some who argue that the Church must be "purged" during the Tribulation to purify it. But this idea is absurd. The blood of Jesus is sufficient to cleanse us of all our sins. That is an accomplished fact for those who have put their faith in Jesus (Ephesians 5:26-27).

To argue that the Church needs purging during the Tribulation is to turn those seven years into a Protestant purgatory!

Some who believe that the Church will go through the Tribulation often point to the example of Noah and his family. They were left on the earth as God poured out His wrath, but they were protected by the Lord. But this example ignores the fact that Enoch was raptured out of the world before the flood began (Genesis 5:24).

Again, I believe Enoch is a symbolic type of the Church and Noah and his family are a type of the Jewish remnant that will be protected through the Tribulation until the day that the Messiah returns.

15 Will the Rapture mark the beginning of the Tribulation?

No, the Bible does not state anywhere that the Tribulation begins with the Rapture.

I believe the Rapture could occur months or even years before the Tribulation begins. However, the Tribulation is likely to start shortly after the Rapture because the Tribulation is the time of the pouring out of God's wrath, and 1 Thessalonians 1:10 says that Jesus will "deliver" His Church "from the wrath to come."

Another reason for believing the Rapture is likely to occur near the beginning of the Tribulation is because 2 Thessalonians 2 says that the Antichrist cannot be revealed until a "restrainer" is "taken out of the way" (2 Thessalonians 2:6-7).

I believe that restrainer is the Holy Spirit working through the Church. Thus, when the Church is removed, the Antichrist will be unleashed, and the Tribulation will begin sometime thereafter, but probably not until the Antichrist has established his power base in Europe.

The prophet Daniel indicates that the starting point of the Tribulation will be a "covenant" that the Antichrist will confirm with Israel that will most likely guarantee the nation's peace and enable the Jews to rebuild their Temple (Daniel 9:27).

16 Are there any other raptures mentioned in the Bible, or is the Rapture of the Church the only one?

Yes, other raptures are mentioned. In fact, the Bible tells about a total of eight.

The first is recorded in Genesis 5:24 where it states that the patriarch, Enoch, "walked with God; and he was not, for God took him." The Bible says he was 365 years old when this took place (Genesis 5:23). So, he was a relatively young man during a time when people lived 800 to 900 years.

What a glorious testimony to the fact that he had such a rich, personal relationship with God that his Creator called him home before his death!

The second biblical rapture was of the prophet Elijah (2 Kings 2:7-14). As his ministry drew to an end, he must have been informed by God that he was going to be taken before he died because he revealed to his disciple, Elisha, that he would soon be "taken" (verse 9).

When informed of this impending event, Elisha requested that a double portion of Elijah's spirit be given to him. Elijah responded by assuring him that if he witnessed his taking, he would receive that blessing. And that is exactly what happened. Elisha witnessed Elijah being taken to heaven in "a chariot of fire and horses of fire" that arose into the heavens like "a whirlwind" (verse 11).

The third rapture mentioned in the Scriptures was a horizontal one whereby Ezekiel was transported by the Spirit from Babylon to Jerusalem where he was shown the idolatry that was taking place in the Temple (Ezekiel 8:1-3).

The fourth rapture is, of course, the ascension of Jesus into Heaven (Acts 1:9-11). This took place 40 days after His resurrection.

And as He was taken up, two angels appeared to the disciples who were witnessing the event and told them that one day Jesus would return "in just the same way as you have watched Him go into heaven" (verse 11). This meant that Jesus would return bodily and visibly.

The next rapture recorded in the Scriptures was another horizontal one. It occurred when the evangelist Philip was transported supernaturally by God from one place to another, following his conversion of an Ethiopian eunuch (Acts 8:26-40).

The Scriptures say that as soon as the Ethiopian was baptized, "the Spirit of the Lord snatched Philip away" (verse 39). The next thing Philip knew, he was in a different locale.

The sixth rapture recorded in the Scriptures is found in 2 Corinthians 12:1-4. In this passage, the Apostle Paul reveals that he was "caught up" to Heaven (verse 2) where he "heard inexpressible words, which a man is not permitted to speak" (verse 4). However, in this case, Paul says he is not sure whether he was taken up in his body or in his spirit (verse 2).

The next example of a biblical rapture is found in the book of Revelation. In chapter 4, the Apostle John says that he was taken up to Heaven to be given a preview of the Tribulation years that would come in the end times (verses 1-2). But, unlike Paul, he says he was definitely in the spirit, so this was not a bodily rapture.

The last rapture recorded in the Scriptures is a future one, like that of the Church, and it will definitely be a bodily one. I have in mind the rapture of the Two Witnesses, who will preach to the world for the first three and a half years of the Tribulation, calling the world to repentance.

Revelation 11 says they will be supernaturally protected by God until the Antichrist goes to Jerusalem in the middle of the Tribulation to declare himself to be god. The Antichrist will kill them and their bodies will lie in the streets of Jerusalem for three and a half days while all the world rejoices over their deaths. Then, suddenly while all the world is watching, they will be resurrected and raptured to Heaven (verses 10-12).

17 What are likely to be some of the world's explanations of the Rapture of the Church?

They will most likely consist of UFO or extraterrestrial scenarios.

The New Age Movement started producing explanations of the Rapture years ago, although they described the event in non-biblical terms.

As far back as the 1970s, New Age leaders were claiming that the "Ascended Masters," (most likely demon angels) with whom they were mystically channeling, had revealed that a day is coming when all those who live by faith will be removed from the planet so that those who live by reason can continue progressing in their evolutionary development toward higher consciousness.[19]

Extraterrestrials (again, demons) are often pictured as the ones who will pull off this great removal of millions of people. And usually they are described as accomplishing the task through the use of UFOs.

The event is often referred to in New Age articles and books as "The Great Evacuation." Other names applied to it are "The Evolutionary Purge," "The Global Cleansing Action," "The Great Shift," and the "Ascension Plan."[20]

Thus, when the Rapture occurs, there is no doubt that the New Age leaders will rush to the microphones and say, "See, we told you many years ago that this was going to happen." And the world will be deceived.

18 Are there any biblical signs we are to watch for that will signal the Rapture of the Church?

No, there are not. This is one of the major differences between the Rapture and the Second Coming.

There are many signs we are told to watch for that will signal the season of the Tribulation and the Second Coming. But since the Rapture is an imminent event, it has been a signless event for the past 2,000 years.

An imminent event is one that can occur at any moment, but that does not necessarily mean it must occur soon. For 2,000 years, the Rapture has been imminent, and thus Christians were urged in the Scriptures to live with an eternal perspective, expecting the Lord to appear at any moment.

What is new is the fact that we now know the Rapture is not only imminent, but that it is also going to happen soon. The reason we can be confident that it is near is because of the signs of the times that are indicating that we are standing on the threshold of the Tribulation.

It's similar to the situation when we see Christmas decorations being put up in stores in September and October. They point to the fact that Christmas is approaching, but they also indicate that Thanksgiving is right around the corner.

The convergence of the signs of the times point to the fact that we are living in the season of the Second Coming, and that means the Rapture is going to happen soon.

19 References are often made to First Century Jewish wedding practices being symbolic of a Pre-Trib Rapture. What is this all about?

There is an amazing symbolic parallel between the stages in a Jewish wedding at the time of Jesus and what the Bible teaches about the relationship of Jesus to His Church and the timing of the Rapture.

Let's consider the various stages and see how they relate to what the Bible teaches concerning Jesus and His relationship to the Church.

1) The Betrothal — The father of the groom would negotiate a wedding covenant or contract that would include the price to be paid for the bride. When the price was paid, the covenant was sealed, and the couple was considered betrothed. Technically, this meant they were married, even though the marriage had not yet been consummated.

In like manner, God the Father sent His Son to the earth to secure a bride (the Church): "For God so loved the world, that He gave His only begotten Son, that whoever believes in Him should not perish, but have eternal life" (John 3:16).

The marriage contract was the "new covenant" referred to in Hebrews 9:15 — "For this reason, He [Jesus] is the mediator of a new covenant, so that, since a death has taken place for the redemption of the transgressions that were committed under the first covenant, those who have been called may receive the promise of the eternal inheritance."

The price for the bride was to be the blood of the Bridegroom, Jesus: " Husbands, love your wives, just as Christ also loved the church and gave Himself up for her . . ." (Ephesians 5:25).

2) The Waiting Period — After the betrothal, there was a waiting period of at least nine months during which the bride and groom were separated.

During this time, the bride prepared herself for the wedding and proved her purity by not becoming pregnant. The groom spent his time preparing a place for them to live, usually by adding a room to his father's house.

In like manner, the Bride of Christ, the Church, is preparing herself today for the union with her Bridegroom by being purified through the Holy Spirit. Thus, in 2 Corinthians 11:2 we read: "For I [the Apostle Paul] am jealous for you with a godly jealousy; for I betrothed you to one husband, so that to Christ I might present you as a pure virgin."

Paul refers to this cleansing process again in Ephesians 5:26-27 where he says that the Lord is sanctifying the Church ". . . by the washing of water with the word, that He might present to Himself the Church in all her glory, having no spot or wrinkle or any such thing; but that she would be holy and blameless."

And just as the First Century Jewish groom spent this waiting period preparing a place for him and his bride to live, Jesus is doing the same today.

In John 14:1-4, Jesus told His disciples at His last supper with them that He was going to return to Heaven to prepare a place for His Bride, the Church. As he put it, "In My Father's house are many dwelling places . . . I go to prepare a place for you" (John 14:2).

3) The Fetching of the Bride — Anytime after the nine month waiting period, when the groom had completed the new living quarters, he would go fetch his bride.

His departure for her would be unannounced, but as he neared her house, he would shout and blow a shofar to alert her to his arrival. Since this was the only warning of his coming, the bride had to be ready at all times for his appearance.

The parallel here with the Rapture of the Church is obvious. The Scriptures say in Luke 12:35 that the Bride of Christ, the Church, must be ready, expecting the Bridegroom to arrive at any time: "Be dressed in readiness, and keep your lamps lit."

The Scriptures also make it clear that when Jesus appears

for His Bride, there will be the shout of an archangel and the blowing of a trumpet (1 Thessalonians 4:16). The Church will then be snatched from the earth and taken to the mansion in Heaven that Jesus has been preparing (John 14:1-4).

4) The Union — Once the Jewish groom fetched his bride in the First Century, he took her to the room he had been preparing where they were cloistered for seven days. It was during this time that the marriage was consummated.

Again, in like manner, the Scriptures tell us that Jesus will take His Bride, the Church, to Heaven where they will remain for seven years (during the time of the Tribulation). The seven years seem to correspond symbolically to the seven days in the bridal chamber.

5) The Celebration — At the end of the seven days in the bridal chamber, the bride and groom would emerge to celebrate their union at an elaborate feast to which their friends were invited.

Likewise, Jesus will celebrate His union with His Bride at the end of the seven years of Tribulation when He hosts what the Bible calls "The Marriage Supper of the Lamb" (Revelation 19:7-9).[21]

Well, as you can see, there is a very definite parallel between the First Century Jewish wedding practices and the marriage of Jesus to His Church. And those parallels clearly point to a Pre-Trib Rapture.

20 **Many people teach that the Rapture will most likely occur on the Jewish Feast of Trumpets, which occurs in the Fall of the year. What is the basis of this belief, and is it accurate?**

The idea is definitely rooted in the Scriptures.

There are seven Jewish feasts each year — four in the Spring and three in the Fall. Each feast has three reference points — past, present and future.

For example, the Feast of Passover (*Pesach* in Hebrew) is a reminder of God's miraculous deliverance of the children of Israel from Egyptian captivity. In the present, it is a celebration of the barley harvest. Concerning the future, it was a prophetic symbol of the Messiah becoming the Passover Lamb who would be sacrificed for the sins of Mankind.

Or, consider the Feast of Harvest, also known as the Feast of Pentecost (*Shavuot* in Hebrew). It points backward to the giving of the Law to Moses at Mount Sinai. In the present, it is a celebration of the wheat harvest. Regarding the future, it proved to be a prophetic symbol of the establishment of the Church, which occurred on the very day of the feast.

The first four feasts have all been prophetically fulfilled with events in the life of Jesus or the history of the Church:

> Passover — The Crucifixion of Jesus
> Unleavened Bread — The Sinless Life of Jesus
> First Fruits — The Resurrection of Jesus
> Pentecost — The Establishment of the Church

We are currently living in the gap between the Spring and Fall feasts — a gap that constitutes the Church Age.

Since the first four feasts were prophetically fulfilled in either the life of Jesus or the history of the Church, it is reasonable to assume that some major events in the history of Christianity will occur in the future on the dates of the three Fall feasts. Usually, the fulfillments are projected as follows:

> Trumpets — The Rapture
> Day of Atonement — The Second Coming
> Tabernacles — The Millennium

The Rapture is associated with the Feast of Trumpets (*Rosh Hashanah* in Hebrew) because it was characterized by the blowing of shofars, and the Rapture will be announced with the sounding of a shofar.

The Second Coming is associated with the Day of Atonement (*Yom Kippur* in Hebrew) because it is a day of repentance for the Jews, and the Scriptures say that a great remnant of the Jews will repent and receive Jesus on the day He returns to earth, at the conclusion of the Tribulation.

The Feast of Tabernacles is the most joyous feast of the year because it signals the completion of the agricultural cycle and thus begins a period of rest. Looking to the past, it is a reminder of the faithfulness of God as He cared for the children of Israel while they were wandering for 40 years in the wilderness, living in temporary booths or tabernacles. But it also looks to the future when the Messiah will come to tabernacle among His people on earth during His millennial reign.

Does this mean that the Rapture will occur some year on the Feast of Trumpets? Perhaps so, but I would not personally make that prediction. I consider the Rapture to be imminent, and that means it could occur at any moment.

21 Does the Bible indicate that there is anything in particular that will trigger the Rapture?

Yes, but it is not a tangible, visible sign that we can be watching for. Rather it is something supernatural.

What I am referring to is mentioned in Romans 11:25, which reads as follows: "For I do not want you, brethren, to be uninformed of this mystery — so that you will not be wise in your own estimation — that a partial hardening has happened to Israel until the fullness of the Gentiles has come in . . ."

I believe this verse is saying that the Rapture will occur when the last Gentile, of the number God has foreordained, is converted to Jesus.

Thus, when that last Gentile convert comes to faith in Christ, the Church — the Body of Christ — will be complete and the Rapture will take place.

The full number of Gentiles will have come in, and then our Lord will turn His attention to the salvation of "all Israel" (Romans 11:26), referring to a Jewish remnant during the subsequent period of the Tribulation.

Near the Cross

A song by Fanny Crosby (1869)
(Public Domain)

Jesus, keep me near the cross,
There a precious fountain —
Free to all, a healing stream —
Flows from Calv'ry's mountain.

Chorus:
In the cross, in the cross,
Be my glory ever;
Till my raptured soul shall find
Rest beyond the river.

Near the cross, a trembling soul,
Love and Mercy found me;
There the Bright and Morning Star
Sheds its beams around me.

Near the cross, O Lamb of God,
Bring its scenes before me;
Help me walk from day to day,
With its shadows o'er me.

Near the cross I'll watch and wait,
Hoping, trusting ever,
Till I reach the golden strand,
Just beyond the river.

Part 3

The Objections

1 The word, rapture, is not even in the Bible. How, then, could the Rapture of the Church be a biblical concept?

This allegation is simply not true because the word can most certainly be found in the Bible.

The word is used in 1 Thessalonians 4:17 in the Latin Vulgate Bible, which was the basic Bible of Western Civilization for 1200 years, from 400 AD to 1611.

Here's how it looks in Latin:

> deinde nos qui vivimus qui relinquimur simul *rapiemur* cum illis in nubibus obviam Domino in aera et sic semper cum Domino erimus

I have highlighted the word, *rapiemur*, which, in English is rendered as "snatched" or "caught up" or "rapture."

So, the word, rapture, is definitely in the Bible. A word does not have to be in English for it to be biblical!

Furthermore, keep in mind that there are many biblical words and concepts that are not mentioned in the Bible in any language — words like Bible, Trinity, Atheism, Divinity, Monotheism, Shekinah Glory, Age of Accountability and Incarnation.

This argument is obviously grasping at straws.

2 The Pre-Trib Rapture concept cannot be true because it was not taught by any of the Church Fathers.

This depends on whom you consider to be the "Church Fathers."

If you are speaking of the biblical Church Fathers — Jesus, Paul, John and Peter — then this allegation holds no water. As I have already shown, all four of these made statements that implied a belief in a Pre-Trib Rapture.

If you are speaking of the non-biblical Church Fathers between about 100 AD and 450 AD, then you are still on thin ice. Although they did not speak specifically of a Rapture of the Church, they did write constantly about the imminence of the Lord's return, a concept that would require a Rapture that is separate from the Second Coming, since there are many prophesied events that must take place before Jesus returns to this earth.

Furthermore, Bible prophecy was not a focus of the writings of these non-biblical Church Fathers, and it is evident from their writings that although they believed in imminence, they had not thought through all the implications of that belief. If they had, they would have seen the need for a truly imminent return that would be separate from the Second Coming.

3 The Pre-Trib Rapture doctrine is too new to be true, since it dates only from the early 1800s.

The opponents of the Pre-Trib Rapture say this because they point to the fact that the theologian who systematized and popularized the concept was John Nelson Darby who lived in England and who first began to fine-tune the concept in 1827.

My first response to this argument is that there are some very good reasons why the doctrine did not develop in its final form until over 1800 years after the establishment of the Church.

Societal Reasons for Delay

For one thing, in the early 5th Century, the Catholic Church adopted Augustine's Amillennial interpretation of end time prophecy as the Church's official eschatological doctrine.[22] That meant that for the next thousand years, if anyone had the audacity to challenge that viewpoint, they were burned at the stake, together with their writings.

So, we really have no idea how many people during that time may have come up with the idea of a Rapture separate and apart from the Second Coming and happening before the Tribulation.

Further, the Catholic Church kept the Bible from the masses. The church argued that only those ordained by the church had the right to interpret the Scriptures.

Also, Bibles had to be produced by hand, and were too expensive for the average person to purchase. And even if they had been available, the average person during the Middle Ages could neither read nor write. So, all they knew about the Bible was what the church shared with them, which was mainly the story of Jesus.

Serious public study of the Bible had to await three developments:

1) The invention of the printing press in 1440, which made it financially feasible to get printed Bibles.

2) The translation of the Bible into the common languages of Europe — like English by William Tyndale and German by Martin Luther.

3) The Reformation in 1517, which broke the domination of the Catholic Church.

And speaking of the Reformation, when Luther had his

confrontation with a Vatican representative at the Diet of
Worms in 1521, he was told that his concept of "salvation by
grace through faith" was "too new to be true" because it
could not be found in the writings of popes, priests or church
fathers.[23]

Luther responded by asserting that his doctrine could be
found in the writings of a far more important person —
namely, the Apostle Paul![24]

A Biblical Reason for Delay

But there is another and more important reason for the
delay in the development of the Pre-Trib Rapture concept,
and it is a biblical one.

The Lord told both Jeremiah and Daniel that many end
time prophecies would not be understood until the time came
for them to be fulfilled (Jeremiah 23:20, Jeremiah 30:24 and
Daniel 12:8-9).

Here's how the Lord expressed this truth to Daniel in
chapter 12 of his book:

> 8) As for me, I heard but could not under-
> stand; so I said, "My lord, what will be the
> outcome of these events?"
>
> 9) He said, "Go your way, Daniel, for these
> words are concealed and sealed up until the
> end time."

The chronological development of a biblical doctrine is
not the true test of its validity. The only true test is whether or
not it is scriptural.

One of the earliest doctrines developed among the Church
Fathers was the concept of salvation by baptism, or "water
regeneration." The fact that it was an early doctrine did not
make it true.

Nor does the recent development of the Pre-Trib doctrine invalidate it. As prophecy scholar Dr. Andy Woods has put it, "Consistency with the Scriptures determines an idea's truthfulness, and not when the idea originated."[25]

A Revealing New Book

A recent book by Dr. William Watson titled *Dispensationalism Before Darby* (2015) has completely destroyed the thesis that the Pre-Trib Rapture doctrine was developed out of the clear blue sky in the 1830s by John Darby.[26]

Dr. William Watson is a professor of history at Colorado Christian University who specializes in 17th and 18th Century English history. He used more than 350 primary sources from those centuries in compiling his new book.

He points out that most of the sources that he quotes in the book have not been previously cited in the debate about the origin of the Pre-Trib Rapture — "most likely because they have not been read for centuries."[27]

Concerning the concept of a Pre-Tribulation Rapture, he concludes that "very little of what John Nelson Darby taught in the mid-nineteenth century was new."[28] His research clearly shows that by the end of the 17th Century, the idea of a Rapture that is separate and apart from the Second Coming had become a commonplace concept.

He identifies six authors who were "clearly Pre-Trib." And he names four who were not Pre-Trib but who refer in their writings to the existence of others who were. He notes that the use of the word, rapture, was also widespread, with some even referring to those who would be "left behind."[29]

Dr. Watson also points out that the interpretation of a Rapture separate and apart from the Second Coming continued to be espoused by Bible prophecy experts throughout the 18th Century. Their timing of the Rapture varied, "but by the end of the 18th Century, *more than a generation before*

Darby, belief in a Rapture of the Church before a great tribulation was commonplace in Britain."[30]

In fact, Dr. Watson demonstrates that "the belief was held not only by Baptists . . . but also by leading Anglicans . . . and even by Scottish Presbyterians . . ."[31]

Without all of Dr. Watson's detailed evidence, secular historian Dr. Paul Boyer had already come to this conclusion in his book, *When Time Shall Be No More; Prophecy Belief in Modern American Culture.*[32] This book was published by Harvard University Press, in 1994. He wrote:[33]

> In a sense, Darby's system contained nothing new. His focus on the future fulfillment of prophecy followed the eschatology of the early Christians. Premillennialism had been an option for Protestant evangelicals since Joseph Mede's day (1586-1639), while rudimentary forms of "Dispensationalism" go back at least as far as Joachim of Fiore (1135-1202).
>
> Even Rapture doctrine . . . can be found in the writings of early interpreters, including Increase Mather (1639-1723). But Darby wove these diverse strands into a tight and cohesive system that he buttressed at every point by copious biblical proof texts, then tirelessly promoted through his writings and preaching tours.

The point is that the concept of a Pre-Trib Rapture did not simply drop from the sky into John Darby's lap in the 1830s. It was a concept that had been slowly developing over several hundred years in the writings of Bible prophecy scholars from a variety of Christian traditions.

4 The modern doctrine of the Pre-Trib Rapture was taken from visions experienced by a teenage Charismatic girl in Scotland named Margaret MacDonald, who was most likely possessed by a demon.

This allegation is total nonsense. The only reason I am addressing it is because it continues to surface.

I came to a belief in a Pre-Trib Rapture through my study of the Scriptures, and it was years later before I ever even heard of Margaret MacDonald.

Todd Strandberg, the founder of the Rapture Ready website, has written, "I cannot recall ever hearing any Pre-Trib speaker say, 'I believe in the Rapture because Margaret MacDonald told me so.'"[34] He goes on to say that he searched all the prophecy books in his library written by those with a Pre-Trib viewpoint, and he could never find even one reference to Margaret MacDonald. He concluded, "It was like looking for the cartoon character, 'Where's Waldo?' Only in this case, no Waldo was to be found."[35]

Personally, I first heard of Margaret MacDonald when a Pre-Trib critic told me that the Pre-Trib Rapture doctrine had to be false because it originated with a teenage Scottish girl who experienced a demonic seizure. That perked my curiosity, so I went searching for this girl, and I found her in a book written by Dave MacPherson in 1973 entitled, *The Unbelievable Pre-Trib Origin*.[36]

Since that time, MacPherson has written at least six subsequent books on the topic, several of which come across as being nothing but the original book with a new title. As one writer has put it, "MacPherson has dedicated his life to full time Rapture hating . . ."[37]

I will never forget how amazed I was when I finished reading MacPherson's book. That's because the book had an appendix that contained Margaret MacDonald's prophetic vision, and I could not find even so much as a hint of a Pre-Trib Rapture in what she supposedly said. Here was a whole book dedicated to the proposition that this girl was the originator of the doctrine, and not one trace of that doctrine could be found in the vision that MacPherson presents as proof!

What is really amazing in this regard is what is contained in a four hour anti-Pre-Trib Rapture video that was produced in 2016 by a ministry in California called "Good Fight Ministries."[38]

From beginning to end, it features the claim that the Pre-Trib Rapture came from Margaret MacDonald. Yet, at one point in the video, the producer looks right into the camera and says: "Our personal position at Good Fight Ministries is that Margaret MacDonald's end time Rapture vision is convoluted, and we can't say for sure that Margaret MacDonald had a partial Pre-Trib Rapture in mind."[39] Duh!

The fact of the matter is that this young woman's vision was about a Post-Tribulation Rapture at the time of the Second Coming, and the only novel things about it were, first, her concept that it would be "secret and invisible," and second, that it would consist of a partial rapture of believers.

The claims concerning the importance of Margaret MacDonald in the development of the Pre-Trib concept of the Rapture are so silly that Todd Strandberg was motivated to write:[40]

> From reading the writings of anti-Rapture authors, one would think we Pre-Tribbers would be reverencing MacDonald as Catholics do Mary. But clearly we don't.

> Pre-Tribbers don't go around reciting, "Hail Margaret full of grace, blessed art thou among visionaries, pray for us sinners at the time of the Rapture."

5 The Pre-Trib Rapture doctrine was conceived by people of questionable character, and therefore it could not possibly be correct.

This is the incredible thesis of the four hour video mentioned above. I call it "incredible" because it consists primarily of an all-out effort to besmirch the reputations of every major person that the producers consider to have played a role in the development of the Pre-Trib Rapture doctrine. In short, the video is four hours of unrelenting character assassination, and as such, it is unbecoming of any Christian ministry.

Personally, I found all this character assassination totally irrelevant to the question of the validity of the Pre-Trib Rapture doctrine. After all, the only people God has to work through here on this earth are sinners.

Using the perverse logic of this objection to the Pre-Trib Rapture, we would also have to dismiss the writings of the Apostle Paul who referred to himself as "the foremost of sinners" (1 Timothy 1:15). And to argue that the sins he referred to were committed before he became a Christian does not alleviate him because after his conversion he wrote that he struggled with sin every day. In Romans 7, he wrote that he often failed to do the good he wished to do: "I practice the very evil that I do not wish" (Romans 7:19).

Likewise, I guess we would have to throw out all of Martin Luther's biblical reforms since he ended up becoming the worst anti-Semite in the history of Christendom.[41] Keep in mind that he wrote a pamphlet near the end of his life in which he provided the blueprint for the Holocaust. This was acknowledged by Hitler in his book, *Mein Kampf*, when he described Luther as a "great warrior, a true statesman, and a great reformer."[42]

All the sleazy character assassination that is contained in this anti-Pre-Trib Rapture video reminded me of the man who is considered to have been the greatest of the Church Fathers. I'm speaking, of course, of Augustine. He holds that honor because his theological ideas had more to do with the shaping of Catholic doctrine than those of any other person.

What most people do not know is that before his conversion, he was a thoroughly immoral person who had devoted his life to debauchery, all of which he details in his famous book called *The Confessions of Augustine*.[43]

Now, I happen to disagree with most of Augustine's theology, and I strongly disagree with all that he taught about Bible prophecy, but I would never attack his doctrines on the basis of his sins. Those are between him and God. The only legitimate basis for attacking anyone's theology is whether or not what they have to say lines up with what the Bible says.

The Bible says God forgives and forgets the sins of those who put their faith in Jesus as Lord and Savior (Hebrews 8:12). The great Christian lady, Corrie ten Boom (1892-1983), used to put it this way: "God has cast our sins in the deepest part of the ocean, and He has put a sign there that reads, 'No Fishing!'"[44]

The deciding point on any theological doctrine should not be who came up with it, but whether or not it passes the test of the Scriptures, and the Pre-Trib Rapture certainly passes that test.

6 **The Church was given the task of preaching the Gospel to the whole world. How can the Church be taken out of the world in a Pre-Trib Rapture before its assigned task is completed?**

This is another of the very strange arguments that is contained in the anti-Pre-Trib Rapture video.

I say this is a strange argument because the Bible never says that the Church will accomplish that task. Rather, it teaches that the task will be accomplished near the end of the Tribulation by an angel who will be sent forth before the final pouring out of God's wrath. This angel will circumnavigate the globe, proclaiming the "eternal Gospel" to "every nation and tribe and tongue and people" (Revelation 14:6).

This argument is rooted in a statement that Jesus made in His Olivet Discourse during the last week of His life. He told His disciples that "This gospel of the kingdom shall be preached in the whole world as a testimony to all the nations, and then the end will come" (Matthew 24:14).

But this is not a requirement for the Rapture to take place. As I have pointed out previously, many souls will be saved during the Tribulation without the presence of the Church. They will be saved through the discovery of Bibles and through the preaching of the 144,000 Jews and the Two Witnesses in Jerusalem. The judgments of the Tribulation will bring some to repentance. So will the Rapture itself.

Then, right at the end of the Tribulation, God in His grace and mercy will send what I call "The Gospel Angel" who will circumnavigate the globe and proclaim the Gospel to every living being in order to give them one last chance to repent and receive Jesus as their Savior. It is this angel, and not the Church that will fulfill Jesus' prophecy in Matthew 24.

7 There is no place in the New Testament where we are specifically told there will be two future comings of the Lord.

This is correct, but two future returns of Jesus are what might be called a "necessary inference."

In like manner, nowhere in the Old Testament is it specifically stated that there will be two future comings of the Messiah. Yet, there is the imagery of Him coming as both a Suffering Lamb and a Conquering Lion — of His dying and His reigning. The necessary inference of these revelations was that there would either be two Messiahs or two comings of the one Messiah.

The vast majority of Jewish sages at the time of Jesus failed to perceive the inference of the Hebrew Scriptures that the Messiah would come twice, including the disciples of Jesus, for which He rebuked them (Luke 24):

> 25) And He said to them, "O foolish men and slow of heart to believe in all that the prophets have spoken!
>
> 26) "Was it not necessary for the Christ to suffer these things and to enter into His glory?"
>
> 27) Then, beginning with Moses and with all the prophets, He explained to them the things concerning Himself in all the Scriptures.

We have the same phenomenon in the New Testament — passages that show the Lord appearing for His Church and other passages revealing Him returning with His Church. These must be reconciled, and, as I have already shown, that cannot be done by concluding that the Rapture and the Second Coming are all one united event.

8 The Bible says that when Jesus returns, all the world will see Him. But the Pre-Trib Rapture doctrine says His appearing in the Rapture will be secret.

Many of the early advocates of a Pre-Trib Rapture referred to it as a "secret," but what they were talking about was misunderstood.

How could the event be a secret when it will propel the whole world into absolute chaos? The reference to it as a "secret" meant that, in their opinion, only believers would see the Lord and hear the shout and the trumpet blast that would herald His appearing.

This terminology is not used anymore because it is so confusing.

As to whether or not believers will be the only ones to see and hear the events associated with the Rapture is a matter of debate. Some believe the event will be like the appearance of Jesus to Paul on the road to Damascus, when he heard Jesus speaking to him, whereas those around him seemed to be able to hear but could not understand what was said (Acts 22:6-9).

It is certainly true that at the Second Coming of Jesus to this earth, "every eye will see Him" (Revelation 1:7).

9 The Pre-Trib Rapture doctrine is an anti-Semitic concept.

I have discovered to my consternation that many Messianic Jews believe that the concept of a Pre-Trib Rapture is an expression of anti-Semitism! They often respond to the idea by saying, "Here we go again, Gentiles getting a free ticket out while the Jews will be left behind to be persecuted and killed."

This attitude is based upon a misunderstanding of the Pre-Trib Rapture doctrine. Many Messianics have the idea that believing Gentiles will be taken out in the Rapture and all Jews will be left behind to suffer the terrors of the Antichrist.

What those with this view fail to understand is that all true believers will be taken out in the Rapture, and that includes Orthodox, Catholic, Protestant, Pentecostal and Messianics. Of course, many who fall into these groups who are not true believers will be left behind. But all true believers, regardless of their label, are members of the Church and are therefore a part of the Bride of Christ.

When Jesus appears in the heavens in the Rapture, he will be coming as a Bridegroom to snatch His Bride out of this world — and that definitely includes Messianics.

Keep in mind also that far more Gentiles than Jews are going to die during the Tribulation. Today there are 7 billion people in the world. If one billion were to be taken in the Rapture, that would leave six billion behind. The Seal Judgments are going to kill one fourth of those (1.5 billion), leaving a total of 4.5 billion (Revelation 6:8). The Trumpet Judgments will kill one-third of those remaining (another 1.5 billion), making a total of 3 billion Gentiles who will die during the first half of the Tribulation. That's one-half the world's population!

Percentage-wise, more Jews will die in the Tribulation. Zechariah 13:8 says two-thirds of them will be killed by the Antichrist. There are approximately 14 million Jews in the world today, so the total number of Jews destined to be killed is about 9.3 million — one-third more than those killed in the Holocaust.

But the point is that unbelieving Jews are not the only ones who are destined to die during the Tribulation. Unbelieving Gentiles are going to experience a mass slaughter that is unparalleled in all of history.[45]

10 People who believe in a Pre-Tribulation Rapture are a bunch of escapists who are not willing to suffer for the Lord.

There is nothing wrong with being an "escapist." Noah was an escapist and so was Lot. And Jesus said that when the end time signs begin to appear, we are to pray "to escape the things that are about to take place and to stand before the Son of Man" (Luke 21:36).

Certainly we are called to suffer for Christ (Romans 8:17). And anyone who truly stands for Jesus in this world will be persecuted (John 15:19). We are assured that as believers we will suffer tribulation in this world (John 16:33), but we are promised that we will be exempted from the Great

Tribulation that will one day come upon all the world (Revelation 3:10).

11 **The Pre-Trib Rapture doctrine produces apathetic Christians who are content with sitting on the sidelines waiting for the Lord's appearing while ignoring evangelism and societal problems.**

This is pure bunk, and yet, it is an accusation that is thrown around constantly.

Let's consider a prime example that will completely discredit this absurd claim. Tim LaHaye was one of the foremost proponents of the Pre-Trib Rapture in the 20th Century. Yet, he encouraged Jerry Falwell to found the Moral Majority, an Evangelical political action group, and was a member of its board of directors.[46] LaHaye's wife, Beverly, founded Concerned Women for America, a conservative Christian women's activist group.[47]

Tim LaHaye also helped establish the Council for National Policy, a political policy-making think tank. He also founded the American Coalition for Traditional Values and the Coalition for Religious Freedom.[48] And while LaHaye was up to his ears in all this political activity, he was writing evangelistic books exhorting people to come to Christ before the Rapture occurs.

The fact of the matter is that those who believe in a Pre-Trib Rapture are anything but apathetic about evangelism and social problems.

They live with an eternal perspective, realizing that the Lord might come at any moment. This expectation motivates them to holiness and evangelism. And as all Christians should, they have a keen concern for societal justice and morality.

12 The Pre-Trib Rapture doctrine will produce a great falling away from the Church when it proves to be false and Christians find themselves in the midst of the Tribulation.

Yes, this could be a problem, if the Pre-Trib Rapture is a false doctrine. But it is not. God has promised that His Son's Bride, the Church, will be immune to the pouring out of His wrath. Our God is faithful to His promises, and we can therefore stand firm that He will honor His promise of deliverance.

And when it happens, it should serve as a powerful motivation for many of those left behind to believe that the Bible really is the Word of God, resulting ultimately in their acceptance of Jesus as their Lord and Savior.

13 Second Thessalonians 2:1-3 says the Church will witness the revealing of the Antichrist, and since the Antichrist will not be revealed until after the Tribulation begins, this means the Church will be in the Tribulation.

At last! A biblical argument against the Pre-Trib Rapture. And it is the cornerstone biblical argument used by those who try to discredit the Pre-Trib doctrine.

Let's take a look at the passage first before we consider the arguments surrounding it. It reads as follows:

> 1) Now we request you, brethren, with regard to the coming of our Lord Jesus Christ and our gathering together to Him,

> 2) that you not be quickly shaken from your composure or be disturbed either by a spirit or a message or a letter as if from us, to the effect that the day of the Lord has come.

> 3) Let no one in any way deceive you, for it

> will not come unless the apostasy comes first,
> and the man of lawlessness is revealed, the
> son of destruction . . .

Now, the argument of those who are determined to discredit the Pre-Trib Rapture is that these verses teach that the Rapture ("our gathering to Him") will not occur until two things take place: the great apostasy and the revelation of the Antichrist. Since the Bible teaches that the Antichrist will not be revealed until the Tribulation begins, this passage means the Church will be on earth during the Tribulation.

The problem is that almost every time the Pre-Trib naysayers quote this passage, they omit the second verse, making it sound like the "it" in verse 3 is referring to the "gathering" in verse 1. But when you read all the verses, it becomes obvious that the antecedent of "it" is really not the "gathering." Instead, it is "the day of the Lord." The gathering refers to the Rapture. The "day of the Lord" refers in this context to the Tribulation and the Millennium.

This passage is actually a very strong proof text for a Pre-Trib Rapture. Paul had obviously taught the Thessalonians about the Rapture and that it would occur before "the day of the Lord," or the beginning of the Tribulation.

But someone had sent them a fake letter from Paul claiming the day of the Lord had begun. Accordingly, they thought they had missed the Rapture! Paul tries to assure them that has not happened because the day of the Lord, the Tribulation, will not begin until the apostasy occurs and the Antichrist is revealed.

It Will Be Worth It All

A song by Esther Kerr Rusthoi
(Public Domain)

Sometimes the day seems long.
Our trials are hard to bear.
We're tempted to complain,
To murmur and despair.
But Christ will soon appear
To catch His Bride away!
All tears forever over
In God's eternal day!

Chorus:
It will be worth it all
When we see Jesus!
Life's trials will seem so small
When we see Christ.
One glimpse of His dear face,
All sorrow will erase.
So, bravely run the race
Til we see Christ.

Part 4

The Conclusion

I have established that God has promised that a day will come when He will remove the Church from this world in an event called the Rapture. There are no ands, ifs or buts about this promise. It is definite. The Rapture has been promised, and it will occur. The main question is, "When?" Is it an imminent event that could occur at any moment? Is it an event separate and apart from the Second Coming? Will it occur before, during or after the Tribulation?

I have tried to prove that the Rapture is an imminent event — one that could occur any moment without any warning — whereas the Second Coming is an event that will be preceded by many signs.

I have tried to demonstrate that although the Rapture is a phase of the Lord's return, it is an event that is definitely separate and apart from the Second Coming.

I have also tried to show that the Rapture will occur before the pouring out of God's wrath in the Tribulation because God has promised to deliver the Church from His wrath.

The Future Blessings of the Pre-Trib Rapture Promise

When the Apostle Paul completed writing his revelation of the Rapture in 1 Thessalonians 4:13-18, he summed it up with this observation: "Therefore, comfort one another with these words."

In what ways should we as believers look upon the promise of the Rapture as a source of comfort? Let me suggest a number of ways.

1) The Rapture promises deliverance from God's wrath.

The signs of the times indicate we are standing on the threshold of the horrendous seven year period of unparalleled violence called the Tribulation (Revelation 6-19).

There is a myth about the Tribulation that many have bought. It is the concept that the first half (3½ years) will be a time of peace, followed by a second half of world-shaking violence. This mistaken concept is based primarily on a statement of Jesus in Matthew 24:21 where He referred to this second half of the Tribulation as the "great tribulation."

But keep in mind that He was speaking to a Jewish audience. With regard to the Jews, it is true that the first half of the Tribulation will be a time of peace and security for them — guaranteed by the Antichrist (Daniel 9:27).

But in the middle of the Tribulation, when the Antichrist comes to Jerusalem and declares himself to be god, the Jewish people will reject him, and he will respond by trying to annihilate them during the second half of the Tribulation (Revelation 12:13-17).

Meanwhile, for the Gentile world, as I have already explained on page 78, the first half of the Tribulation will result in the deaths of half their worldwide population. It will be a slaughter of unparalleled proportions.

The Antichrist is going to rise to power in Europe through deceit and diplomatic cunning, but he will expand his rule over the whole world through wars of unprecedented violence.

The Pre-Trib Rapture promises us deliverance from this insane bloodbath. There is just no purpose for the Church to be present on the earth during the Tribulation.

2) The Rapture promises resurrection for those who have died in Christ.

The dead in Christ will not be left behind when the Church is taken from this world, as the Christians in the church at Thessalonica feared they might be. In his detailed explanation of the Rapture, Paul assured the Thessalonian church that their loved ones who had died as believers in Jesus would be resurrected and would go up first to meet the Lord in the sky — even before those who would be alive at the time.

This was, of course, a great source of comfort to the living descendants of those believers who had died. It continues to be so to this day. Tim LaHaye explained this when he told about his response to his father's death.

Tim was only 9 years old at the time when his father died suddenly of a heart attack. He described his response in this way:[49]

> I was devastated. I wept until I had no more tears, and could not be comforted until we arrived at the cemetery.
>
> The minister who conducted the service had led my parents to Christ six years earlier. I will never forget the moment when he put his hand on the casket and said, based on Paul's great passage [about the Rapture], "The world has not heard the last of Frank LaHaye."
>
> Then, pointing to the heavens, he said, "The day is coming when Jesus will shout from heaven, and the dead [in Christ] will rise from their graves and will be transformed . . . and together we will be taken up to be with Jesus in the Rapture."

As the pastor was speaking, he pointed upward, and suddenly, some sunlight burst through an opening in that overcast Michigan sky and entered my young heart. That was the first time I realized that one day I would see my father again! On that day, the "blessed hope" of Christ's return for His children was born into me and has never left.

3) The Rapture promises the living an escape from death.

I have always heard there are two things no one can escape: death and taxes.

That is wrong, because there is a whole generation that will not taste death — namely, the believers in Jesus who are alive at the time of the Rapture.

They will be snatched up to Jesus, and on the way up to meet Him, they will be transformed from mortal to immortal (1 Corinthians 15:42, 50-55).

4) The Rapture promises the gift of glorified bodies.

Our translation from mortal to immortal means no more aging, pain or suffering.

The lame will walk, the deaf will hear, the mute will speak and the mentally impaired will have their minds set right.

I have an adult step-grandson named Jason who has lived in a padded room for almost 30 years. He also has to wear a helmet to protect himself when he bangs his head against the wall. He has no idea who he is, where he is, or who anyone else is. I look forward to the day of the Rapture when his mind will be healed, and I will be able to talk with him and enjoy his fellowship forever.

The Current Blessings
of the Rapture Promise

The promise of the Rapture not only provides blessings we can look forward to in the future, it also provides some very real blessings in the present.

This is a point I emphasize over and over to pastors who see no relevance of Bible prophecy to the here and now. Instead, they tend to view it as just pie-in-the-sky promises related to the distant future.

Our churches are filled with people who believe in the Second Coming intellectually, but not with their hearts, and therefore, their belief has no impact on the way they live. It is only when you convict Christians in their hearts of two prophetic truths that you will transform the way they live:

1) That Jesus really is going to return.

2) That this event could occur at any moment.

These life-transforming convictions can only come from a belief in a Pre-Trib Rapture because it motivates people to live with a sense of imminence, expectancy and urgency. Or, to put it another way, it promotes living with an eternal perspective.

And the development of such an attitude motivates, in turn, two commitments that can transform the lives of individual believers as well as the life of a church. For a genuine belief in a Pre-Trib Rapture will motivate holiness and evangelism.

What more could any pastor desire than a congregation full of members who are committed to holy living and evangelism?

Another current blessing of the Pre-Trib Rapture promise is that it provides hope — incredible hope.

Jesus prophesied that the world would once again become as evil as it was in the day of Noah, and He said this would be an indicator of when He would return (Matthew 24:37). We are witnessing that prophecy being fulfilled before our very eyes, and we need hope. The promise of the Pre-Trib Rapture provides that hope.

The great pastor, Adrian Rogers (1931-2005), had that hope. He believed in the signs of the times and the Rapture, and because of those beliefs, he once proclaimed, "The world is growing gloriously dark." Glorious because the increasing darkness points to the end of the end times and that, in turn, indicates that the Rapture is closer than ever before.[50]

In a similar way, Jan Markell, the founder of Olive Tree Ministries, often says, "The world is not falling to pieces. Rather, the pieces are all falling into place."[51]

The Church's Prophetic Need

The Church desperately needs a sense of imminency because the signs of the times point to the fact that we are living on borrowed time.

Again, we are on the very threshold of the Tribulation, which, in turn, means that *the Rapture is now more than just imminent. It is immediate.*

Consider for a moment the many end time signs we are told to watch for. There are so many that the only way I have ever been able to get a handle on them is to organize them into six categories:[52]

1) The Signs of Nature

2) The Signs of Society

3) The Spiritual Signs

4) The Signs of Technology

5) The Signs of World Politics

6) The Signs of Israel

The provision of so many end time signs in the Bible is proof positive that God wants the end time generation to be fully aware that it is living in the season of His Son's return. The reason, of course, is that God in His grace and mercy does not wish that any should be lost, but that all might come to repentance before it is too late (2 Peter 3:9).

Amazingly, the most important end time sign is not included in any of the categories listed above. It is the over-reaching sign of CONVERGENCE. What it refers to is the fact that all the signs of the end times are converging for the first time ever.

God is about to pour out His wrath on this sin-sick, re-bellious world, and He is shouting that intention from the heavens, by using prophetic voices to point us to the signs of the times.[53] Our remaining time is short. And there is a crucial question each one of us must face.

The Crucial Question

Are you ready? Are you prepared for the appearance of Jesus for His Church? Will you be taken in the Rapture, or will you be left behind to face the horrors of the Tribulation and the terror of the Antichrist? Will the appearance of Jesus in the heavens for His Church be your blessed hope or your holy terror?

Maybe you are thinking, "I probably would go because I was born into a Christian family." Or maybe your feeling is, "I'm almost positive I would go because I was baptized as a kid, and I've attended church at least once a year since then."

Or perhaps you are one of the majority of people who re-spond to this question by saying, "Well, I've never been very religious, and I don't go to church, but I'm not a bad person, and I am certainly a lot better than most of the people I know — I mean, I'm not caught up in any serious sins."

If any of these thoughts are yours, then you need to face up to some grim realities:

- You cannot be saved by being born into a Christian family.

- You cannot be saved by performing certain religious rituals.

- You cannot be saved by performing good works.

- You cannot be saved by avoiding certain major sins.

- You cannot be saved by living better than your neighbor.

- You cannot be saved by joining a church.

Jesus said the only way anyone can be saved is for them to be "born again" (John 3:3). What does that mean? It refers to spiritual rebirth.

The Consequence of Our Sins

Our sins have resulted in our spiritual death. The Bible puts it this way, "The wages of sin is death" (Romans 6:23). We must be spiritually reborn in order to be reconciled to God and have the hope of everlasting life with Him.

How can you experience that spiritual rebirth? By placing your faith in Jesus as your Lord and Savior. That's the only way. Jesus Himself defined salvation as a personal relationship with Him when He said, "This is eternal life, that they may know You, the only true God, and Jesus Christ whom You have sent" (John 17:3).

This vital point makes true Christianity a matter of a relationship, rather than a religion. Religion does not save. Only Jesus saves. Jesus made this crystal clear when He declared, "I am the way, and the truth, and the life; no one comes to the Father but through Me" (John 14:6).

Why Jesus?

God's Word, the Bible, says Jesus was God in the flesh (Matthew 1:23, John 10:30 and 1 John 5:20). It also says that He lived a perfect, sinless life (Hebrews 4:15 and 2 Corinthians 5:21). That means He is the only person who has ever lived who did not deserve to die, for "the wages of sin is death" (Romans 6:23).

Thus, when Jesus voluntarily went to the cross to suffer and die the most horrible of deaths, He did so, not for His sins, but for yours and mine. Paul expressed it this way in 1 Corinthians 15:3: "For I delivered to you as of first importance what I also received, that Christ died for our sins according to the Scriptures . . ." Peter affirmed this statement in 1 Peter 3:18 when he wrote: "For Christ also died for sins once for all, the just for the unjust, so that He might bring us to God, having been put to death in the flesh, but made alive in the spirit . . ."

This means that when Jesus was hanging on the cross, every sin you and I have ever committed and ever will commit was placed upon Him, and He received the wrath of God, which you and I deserve. When you accept Jesus as your Lord and Savior, you step into the area where the wrath of God has already fallen, and you become immune to that wrath.

There is a contemporary Christian song that powerfully expresses this truth. It says:[54]

> He paid a debt He did not owe;
> I owed a debt I could not pay;
> I needed someone to wash my sins away.
> And, now, I sing a brand new song,
> "Amazing Grace"
> Christ Jesus paid a debt that I could never pay.

Another Crucial Question

This brings us to a key question: How do we appropriate the blood of Jesus to our lives so that we can receive forgiveness of sins, the hope of the Rapture and eternal life with God?

The Bible's answer is that salvation is a free gift of God's grace, which we receive through Jesus by responding to Him in faith (Romans 5:1-2). Here's how Paul put it in Ephesians 2:8 — "For by grace you have been saved through faith; and that not of yourselves, it is the gift of God."

God's plan of salvation has always been the same — grace through faith. Before the Cross, the focal point of that faith was God the Father and His promise of a Messiah. Since the Cross, the focal point of saving faith has been God the Son, Jesus the Messiah, who died for our sins.

The Faith That Saves

Notice that in the previous sentence I used the term, "saving faith." That term was carefully selected because the faith that saves is something far more substantial than a simple belief that Jesus was the Christ, the Son of the living God. After all, the Scriptures say that "even the demons believe and tremble" (James 2:19).

Saving faith produces trust in Jesus as one's Savior (John 3:16-17). The faith that saves also produces obedience to God's Word (1 John 5:3). And true saving faith is always manifested in good works (Ephesians 2:10).

The latter point is a paradox. We are not saved by good works. Rather, we are saved to do good works (Titus 2:14). We don't work to be saved. We work because we are saved. True faith will always be manifested in works, "for faith without works is dead" (James 2:14-26).

The True Meaning of Salvation

This brings us back to the essence of salvation. I want to emphasize once again that it is a relationship with a Man and not obedience to a plan. We become saved by putting our trust in a person, and we remain saved by continuing to trust in that person.

That person, of course, is Jesus of Nazareth who was God in the flesh (John 1:1-14). That is why Jesus said, "I am the way, and the truth, and the life; no one comes to the Father, but through Me" (John 14:6). It is also the reason that Jesus said, "This is eternal life, that they know You, the only true God, and Jesus Christ whom You have sent" (John 17:3).

The essence of Christianity is a relationship with a person. You enter that relationship by an act of faith whereby you accept Jesus as your Lord and Savior.

> Without faith it is impossible to please God, for he who comes to God must believe that He is, and that He is a rewarder of those who seek Him (Hebrews 11:6).

If you have never put your faith in Jesus as your Lord and Savior, I invite you to do so now. Confess to God that you are a sinner and ask Him to forgive you of your sins. And then receive Jesus as your Savior.

Once you have done this, seek out a Bible-believing church where Jesus is exalted as the only Hope for the world. Go before that church and confess your faith and then manifest that faith in water baptism. Then, seek out a Bible study and prayer group within that church where you can begin to grow in your faith.

Having done this, you will be ready for the return of the Lord, and you can join with me and many other Christians who welcome each day with great hope by exclaiming, "Maranatha! Come quickly, Lord Jesus" (1 Cor. 16: 22).

What About Believers?

What about those of us who have already received Jesus as our Lord and Savior? How should we prepare for the Rapture of the Church?

This question is answered by the Apostle Paul in Titus 2:

> 11) For the grace of God has appeared, bringing salvation to all men,
>
> 12) instructing us to deny ungodliness and worldly desires and to live sensibly, righteously and godly in the present age,
>
> 13) looking for the blessed hope and the appearing of the glory of our great God and Savior, Christ Jesus,
>
> 14) who gave Himself for us to redeem us from every lawless deed, and to purify for Himself a people for His own possession, zealous for good deeds.

In this passage, Paul begins in verse 11 by referring to the First Coming of Jesus as a manifestation of "the grace of God," providing salvation to a world that did not deserve it.

In verse 12 and 13, he begins to tell us what we as believers should be doing as we await the "blessed hope" — his term for the Rapture. He says we are to:

- Deny ungodliness,
- Deny worldly desires,
- Live sensibly, righteously and godly,
- And live with an eternal perspective by looking daily for the appearing in glory of Jesus.
- We are also to seek to do good deeds that will bring honor and glory to Jesus.

The Apostle John emphasized the importance of living with an eternal perspective when he wrote in 1 John 3:

> 2) Beloved, now we are children of God, and it has not appeared as yet what we will be. We know that when He appears, we will be like Him, because we will see Him just as He is.
>
> 3) And everyone who has this hope fixed on Him purifies himself, just as He is pure.

In other words, if believers will live with an eternal perspective, yearning for the appearing of Jesus for His Church, they will experience increasing spiritual purification.

They will also become candidates for a special reward when they stand before the judgment seat of Jesus. Paul makes this promise in 2 Timothy 4:8 where he says that a "crown of righteousness" will be given to each believer who lived his life looking forward to the "appearing" of Jesus.

If you are a believer, are you a candidate for that reward? I hope so.

Maranatha!

Blessed Assurance

A song by Fanny Crosby (1873)
(Public Domain)

Blessed assurance, Jesus is mine!
Oh, what a foretaste of glory divine!
Heir of salvation, purchase of God,
Born of His Spirit,
Washed in His blood.

Chorus:
This is my story, this is my song,
Praising my Savior all the day long;
This is my story, this is my song,
Praising my Savior all the day long.

Perfect submission, perfect delight,
Visions of Rapture now burst on my
    sight;
Angels descending, bring from above
Echoes of mercy, whispers of love.

Perfect submission, all is at rest.
I in my Savior am happy and blest,
Watching and waiting,
Looking above,
Filled with His goodness,
Lost in His love.

About the Author

D r. David R. Reagan founded Lamb & Lion Ministries in 1980 after spending 20 years as a professor of international law and politics. He is a Phi Beta Kappa graduate of the University of Texas in Austin. He earned his graduate degrees from The Fletcher School of Law and Diplomacy — a school of international studies that is owned and operated jointly by Tufts and Harvard Universities.

Dr. Reagan is a lifelong student of the Bible. Since 1980 he has held Bible prophecy seminars all over the United States and around the world. He is the host of a weekly television program called *Christ in Prophecy* that is broadcast over many national Christian networks, regional networks and stations, and a variety of Christian websites. It is also broadcast over satellites around the world. Additionally he serves as the editor of the ministry's bi-monthly *Lamplighter* magazine.

One of Dr. Reagan's specialties is the Middle East and its role in end time prophecy. He has been to Israel more than 45 times.

Dr. Reagan and his wife, Ann, have been married almost 60 years. They reside in a suburb of Dallas, Texas. They are the parents of two daughters, and they have 4 grandchildren and 2 great grandchildren.

Lamb & Lion Ministries is a non-denominational ministry dedicated to the teaching of Bible prophecy and the proclamation of the Lord's soon return. The ministry's website can be found at www.lamblion.com.

There Ain't No Grave
Gonna Hold This Body Down!

A song by Claude Ely
(Public Domain)

You can take me to the grave yard,
And you can lay this old body down,
But on that first resurrection morning,
I'm gonna come up, come up, come up outta
    the ground.

Chorus:
There ain't no grave gonna hold my body down.
There ain't no grave gonna hold my body down.
'Cause when I hear that trumpet sound,
I'm gonna get up, get up, get up outta the ground.
There ain't no grave gonna hold my body down.

Oh yes and meet me, Jesus, meet me
Meet me in the middle of the air.
And if these wings don't fail me, Lord,
I know that you'll be there.

References

Preface

1) Recommended books that cover the Rapture in great detail include the following: *When the Trumpet Sounds* edited by Thomas Ice and Timothy Demy (Eugene, OR: Harvest House, 1995); *The Popular Handbook on the Rapture,* edited by Tim LaHaye, Thomas Ice and Ed Hindson (Eugene, OR: Harvest House, 2011); *The Rapture: Don't Be Deceived,* by Billy Crone (Las Vegas, NV: Get A Life Publications, 2016); and *Can We Still believe in the Rapture?* by Ed Hindson and Mark Hitchcock (Eugene, OR: Harvest House, 2017).

Part 1: The Concept

2) David Reagan, *Trusting God: Learning How to Walk by Faith,* Third Edition (McKinney, TX: Lamb & Lion Ministries, 2015).

3) *Rapture- Palooza,* a motion picture by Mimran Schur Pictures, 2013.

4) Mark Woods, "Why A Zombie Invasion Is More Likely Than A Religious Apocalypse," *Christian Today* magazine, October 3, 2016, www.christiantoday.com/article/why-a-zombie-invasion-is-more-likely-than-a-religious-apocalypse/96977.htm.

5) Gary Demar, "Jan Markell's End-Time Hysteria Conference," July 29, 2013, https://garydemar.com/jan-markells-end-time-hysteria-conference.

6) Dean C. Halverson, "88 Reasons: What Went Wrong?" *Christian Research Journal,* Fall 1988, www.equip.org/article/88-reasons-what-went-wrong.

7) Harold Camping, *1994?* (New York: Vantage Press. 1992).

8) Harold Camping, *Time Has An End,* (Alameda, CA: Family Station, Inc, 2005).

9) David Reagan, *Eternity: Heaven or Hell?* (McKinney, TX: Lamb & Lion Ministries, 2010).

Part 2: The Questions

10) David Reagan, *Wrath and Glory: Unveiling the Majestic Book of Revelation* (Green Forest, AR: New Leaf Press, 2001). Second edition in 2016 by Lamb & Lion Ministries.

11) Ron Rhodes, "The Rapture: Pre, Mid, Late or Post Trib?" Contained in the audio album, *The Great Debates of Bible Prophecy: 2016 Bible Conference*, produced by Lamb & Lion Ministries.

12) Tommy Ice, "The Rapture in 2 Thessalonians 2:3?" www.rapture ready.com/2015/11/10/the-rapture-in-2-thessalonians-23-by-thom as-ice.

13) Jim Tetlow, "The Rapture in the Old Testament," *Lamplighter* magazine of Lamb & Lion Ministries, July-August 2012, pages 9-10.

14) David Reagan, *Eternity: Heaven or Hell?* (McKinney, TX: Lamb & Lion Ministries, 2010).

15) Jack Van Impe, "Could there be a 'partial' Rapture?" JVI email newsletter, September 23, 2013, www.jvim.com/september-23-2013, page 1.

16) Ibid.

17) J. B. Phillips, *The New Testament in Modern English* (New York: The Macmillan Co., 1958).

18) *New Living Translation* (Carol Stream, IL: Tyndale House Publishers, 2015). Although this version of the Bible claims to be a "dynamic equivalence" translation, it is really more of a paraphrase.

19) Koinonia House eNews Letter, "How Will the World Explain the Rapture?" April 9, 2013, www.khouse.org/enews_article/2013/2068.

20) David J. Stewart, "The Rapture According to New Age Channelers," www.jesus-is-savior.com/False%20Religions/New%20Age/newage-rapture.htm.

21) Some Bible prophecy experts whom I highly respect teach that the Marriage Feast of the Lamb, which is recorded in Revelation 19:7-9, will be held on earth *after* the return of Jesus — despite the fact that this event is clearly pictured as being held in Heaven *before* the Second Coming. Their argument seems to be based primarily on a statement in Luke 22:28-30 where Jesus promises believers that they will "eat and drink at My table in My kingdom . . ." This

statement certainly leaves the impression that the feast will be held after the Lord returns and establishes His kingdom here on this earth. Additionally, some point to Luke 13:28-30 where Jesus says that the saved will one day "come from east and west, and from north and south, and will recline at the table in the kingdom of God." They conclude their argument by pointing to Isaiah 25:6, which is a Millennial setting and which refers to a "lavish banquet for all peoples on this mountain" — referring to Mount Zion in Jerusalem (Isaiah 24:23). As you can see, the argument in behalf of the Marriage Feast being held here on earth is certainly grounded in the Scriptures, but I believe the conclusion is unwarranted. That's because I believe the Bible is prophesying two great feasts in the end time. The first will be the Marriage Feast of the Lamb in Heaven when Jesus will celebrate His union with His Bride, the Church. The second banquet, which I call The Zion Feast, will take place here on earth in Jerusalem after the return of Jesus. It will include Old Testament Saints and Tribulation Martyrs as well as Church Age Saints. Its purpose will be to celebrate the Lord's return and the inauguration of His Millennial Kingdom.

Part 3: The Objections

22) New World Encyclopedia contributors, "Amillennialism," *New World Encyclopedia,* November 17, 2016, www.newworldencyclopedia.org/entry/Amillennialism.

23) Andy Woods, "The Rapture, Part 10," February 6, 2013, www.bibleprophecyblog.com/2013/02/the-rapture-part-10.html, page 3.

24) Ibid.

25) Ibid., page 2.

26) William Watson, *Dispensationalism Before Darby* (Silverton, OR: Lampion Press, 2015).

27) Ibid., page 177.

28) Ibid.

29) Ibid., pages 177-178.

30) Ibid., page 262.

31) Ibid.

32) Paul Boyer, *When Time Shall Be No More: Prophecy Belief in Modern American Culture* (Boston: Harvard University Press, 1994).

33) Ibid., page 88.

34) Todd Strandberg, "Margaret MacDonald Who?" www.rapture ready.com/rr-margaret-macdonald.html, page 1.

35) Ibid.

36) Dave MacPherson, *The Unbelievable Pre-Trib Origin*, (Kansas City, MO: Heart of America Bible Study, 1973).

37) Rapture Ready, "Dave MacPherson: Inventor of False Pre-Trib Rapture History," www.raptureready.com/dave-macpherson, page 1.

38) Joseph Schimmel, *Left Behind or Led Astray?* A video program produced by Good Fight Ministries, Simi Valley, California, 2015. www.goodfight.org/product/left-behind-or-led-astray.

39) Ibid., Disc 1 at 1:37:45.

40) Strandberg, "Margaret MacDonald Who?" page 1.

41) Martin Luther, *On The Jews and Their Lies* (1543), www.prchiz .pl/pliki/Luther_On_Jews.pdf.

42) Adolph Hitler, *Mein Kampf*, volume 1 (1925), chapter VIII.

43) Saint Augustine, *Confessions,* translated by R.S. Pine-Coffin (New York: Penguin Books, 1961).

44) Debbie McDaniel, "40 Powerful Quotes from Corrie ten Boom," www.crosswalk.com/faith/spiritual-life/inspiring-quotes/40-powerful-quotes-from-corrie-ten-boom.html.

45) Two Messianic Jewish authors have presented strong arguments in behalf of the Pre-Trib Rapture: Arnold Fruchtenbaum, *The Footsteps of the Messiah* (Tustin, CA: Ariel Ministries, 1982) and Richard Hill, *Israel in Prophecy: A Chronology* (Maitland, FL: Xulon Press, 2018).

46) Wikipedia, "Tim LaHaye," https://en.wikipedia.org/wiki/Tim_ La Haye.

47) Wikipedia, "Beverly LaHaye," https://en.wikipedia.org/wiki/ Beverly_LaHaye.

48) Wikipedia, "Tim LaHaye."

Part 4: Conclusion

49) Tim LaHaye, Thomas Ice and Ed Hindson, editors, *The Popular Handbook on the Rapture,* (Eugene, OR: Harvest House, 2011),

page 51.

50) Bob Russell, "Longing for His Appearing," a presentation at the 2015 Lamb & Lion Annual Bible Conference. Contained in the conference video album, *Messages for a Rebellious Nation* (Lamb & Lion Ministries, 2015).

51) Jan Markell, "The Mockery of Bible Prophecy," a presentation at the 2018 Lamb & Lion Annual Bible Conference. Contained in the conference video album, *God's Prophetic Voices to America* (McKinney, TX: Lamb & Lion Ministries, 2018).

52) David Reagan, *Living on Borrowed Time: the Imminent Return of Jesus* (McKinney, TX: Lamb & Lion Ministries, 2013).

53) David Reagan, *God's Prophetic Voices to America* (McKinney, TX: Lamb & Lion Ministries, 2017).

54) Ellis J. Crum, "He Paid A Debt He Did Not Owe," www.touch jesussongs.net/lyricspage15.html.

"The Bible says that believers in the last generation will not experience physical death, but will be caught up in what is called the 'Rapture' — the 'snatching away' to meet Jesus in the air and be reunited with loved ones who have died in Christ and have gone before us. It will be the trip of a lifetime — a trip that is out of this world. Are you ready?" — Anne Graham Lotz, daughter of Billy Graham and head of Angel Ministries. ("Are Your Ready for the Rapture?" *Decision* magazine, April 24, 2017.)

Rapture Video

In 2016, a ministry in California produced a very mean-spirited 4½ hour video that attacked the validity of the concept of a Pre-Trib Rapture. The video relied on character assassination and was filled with misrepresentations concerning what the Bible teaches about the timing of the Rapture.

This one hour and 32 minute video is Dr. Reagan's response. Rather than focusing on individuals, this response concentrates on biblical arguments in behalf of the concept that the Rapture is most likely to occur before the Tribulation begins.

Dr. Reagan believes this is one of the most important videos that the ministry has ever produced. It not only presents a firm biblical case for a Pre-Trib Rapture, it also deals with many of the silly myths about the doctrine that have been conjured up by the opponents.

One of the highlights of the video is that it features interviews with Tommy Ice, Andy Woods, Mark Hitchcock, William Watson, Charles Ryrie, and Tim LaHaye.

This video program is available for $20, including the cost of shipping. To order, call 972-736-3567 between 8am and 5pm Central time, Monday through Friday. You can also place your order through the ministry's website at www.lamblion.com.

Many other Rapture study resources are available at the Lamb & Lion website, including videos, TV programs and books. You can also find articles from past issues of the ministry's *Lamplighter* magazine. The site has a high-speed search engine that you can use to quickly locate resource materials about any subject in the field of Bible prophecy. ❖